# Common BIRDS

of

# Washington & Oregon

J. Duane Sept

*Calypso Publishing*

National Library of Canada Cataloguing in Publication Data

Sept, J. Duane, 1950-
    Common birds of Washington & Oregon / J. Duane Sept.

    Includes bibliographical references and index.
    ISBN 0-9730390-3-5 1.

    Birds--Washington (State)--Identification. 2. Birds--Oregon--Identification. I. Title.
QL684.06S46 2003        598'.09795        C2003-910328-5

Front Cover Photo: Bald eagle by J. Duane Sept.
Back Cover Photos: Great blue heron, barn swallow and birdwatchers by J. Duane Sept.
Printing: Kromar Printing Ltd., Winnipeg, MB, Canada.

Published by:
**Calypso Publishing**
P.O. Box 1141
Sechelt, BC Canada
V0N 3A0

**Website:** http://www.calypso-publishing.com

# Table of Contents

# Quick Photo Guide to the Bird Groups

Loons                    p. 14

Grebes                   p. 15

Cormorants               p. 16

Herons                   p. 17

Swans                    p. 18

Geese                    p. 19

Ducks                    p. 21

Eagles & Hawks           p. 32

Falcons                  p. 37

Grouse & Allies   p. 38

Rails                    p. 41

Cranes                   p. 42

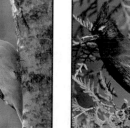

# Welcome to Birding

The pursuit of observing birds has become one of the fastest growing recreational activities in North America, from a casual and occasional pastime to an intense passion. Birding can be enjoyed in urban and rural settings and at any time of year—spring, summer, fall and winter. Some birders have life lists and many participate in Christmas bird counts as well as breeding bird surveys. Still others plan their vacations around good birding locations.

The sights and sounds of our winged wonders bring pleasure to all, young and old, and a great deal of interesting information has been discovered about our birds and their behaviors. This book will help all birders to understand the magnificent free-fliers of the Pacific Northwest.

# How to Use This Book

The birds in this book are arranged in order of evolutionary sequence, the method that is used in most bird references. This order is quickly learned and makes it easier for the novice to find specific groups of birds, such as ducks, in other books about birds.

The quick photo guide on p. 4 will aid you in finding the main bird groups and narrowing your search.

## Parts of A Bird

eyebrow
Crown
lore
nape
chin
eye-line
throat
rump
breast
upper tail coverts
wing bars
secondary feathers
primary feathers

Savannah sparrow.

## Species Information and Identifying Features

Color photographs, descriptions and concise information are included for each bird.

**NAME:** The current accepted common name and scientific or Latin name.

**DESCRIPTION** The most distinguishing physical features, to aid in identification.

**SIZE** Dimensions for large individuals of the species.

**NESTING** Nest site and materials, along with usual number and color of eggs.

**HABITAT** The type of area where the species lives, sometimes with added information if there are seasonal habitats.

Natural history notes are included for each species, offering interesting information on behavior, populations or special characteristics.

**Similar Species:** Distinguishing features of similar birds.

# Tips and Techniques for Better Birding

## Birdsong

Although birding can be conducted at any time of the day, the best time to observe many species, during the breeding season, is early morning while the males are singing. Listen for birdsong, since many species have distinctive calls and songs. It is possible to identify many species by voice before you can see them. This is especially true during the spring and summer, and, for some species, during the entire year.

# Calling

One technique that often brings birds closer, so that you can get a better view, is to call them. Try making a repeated "swishing" sound. Other calls such as *pishh* and *Sip! Sip! Sip!* can also be effective, as well as noises made by squeaking the back of the hand in a sort of "kissing" sound. This technique should not be used excessively in one area, as it can stress breeding birds.

Some smaller bird species are sometimes affectionately referred to as "little brown jobs" (LBJs) if they cannot be identified. Sandpipers, which can also be difficult to identify, are sometimes referred to as "peeps."

# Choosing Equipment

### Binoculars

Binoculars are an excellent tool for observing all birds. They do not have to be large or heavy—they should be powerful enough to magnify the subject sufficiently but should not be too difficult to hold steady. Binoculars are rated by both their magnification and light-gathering abilities. A pair of binoculars with a rating of 7 x 40 can magnify the subject 7 times or 700%. If you are looking for your first pair of binoculars, I recommend that you choose a pair with a wide range of vision. This will aid you greatly in getting the bird in view, a skill that takes practice to learn. A pair of binoculars with 10 power, for example, may have too narrow a field of vision for beginning birders.

The second number in the designation—40, in the 7 x 40 binoculars—is the diameter of the objective lens (in millimeters) where the light enters. The larger this number, the more light is available for viewing in low-light situations, including dusk and dawn. A good beginning pair of binoculars for birding is 7 x 35 or 7 x 40. Higher magnifications and light-gathering abilities are excellent for a second pair, once you have experience at finding the birds in your binoculars. Low-light conditions may not apply at the time of day when you are observing birds.

Be sure to talk to others about the advantages and disadvantages of their binoculars. A good way to do this is to join an outdoor club. The more you can try out various binoculars in the field, the more informed choice you will be able to make.

## Spotting Scopes

Many serious birding enthusiasts use spotting scopes, because they make it possible to see more details of a bird at greater distances. A tripod or car window can be used to steady this excellent tool. Magnification begins at approximately 20 times. Excellent zoom optics are available, with which you can zero in on your subject. Spotting scopes are more costly than many binoculars, depending upon quality, magnification capability and brand.

# Virtual Birding Sites

Several web sites are available to help birders find and observe birds. The following sites were available at the time this book was written (March 2003).

The Bird Guide: Your guide to birds and birding in the Pacific Northwest
http://thebirdguide.com/

Backyard Birdwatching Almanac
http://www.suite101.com/linkcategory.cfm/10080/25542

Virtual Birder (Rare Bird Alerts)
http://www.virtualbirder.com/vbirder/realbirds/index.html

Birding in BC
http://birding.bc.ca/

North American Bird Sounds
http://www.naturesongs.com/birds.html

Washington Ornithological Society
http://www.wos.org/WOSLinks.htm

Oregon Hotspots
http://www.camacdonald.com/birding/usoregon.htm

# Maps

**British Columbia**

**Washington & Oregon**

# Attracting Birds to Your Home

## Food

Giving birds a nutritious meal is an excellent way to bring them close to your home and garden and to experience the wonders of nature. Many people think that if ducks or other birds eat bread or crackers, it must be OK to give it to them. But no birds should be fed bread, crackers, chips or similar foods meant for people. These items have no nutritional value, so they actually rob the birds of the nourishment they need to migrate or to survive the winter. A variety of wild bird seed is available at specialty stores.

It is very gratifying to attract birds year-round and observe them on a regular basis. Select foods that are appropriate for the species you wish to attract. Place your feeder at a site where you can observe the birds but not startle them while they feed. Elevate the feeding area so that the birds can watch for predators, including domestic cats, and place it away from cover such as trees, to prevent cats from capturing "your" birds. At times, hawks and owls may also frequent a feeder, to find an easy meal.

## Birdhouses

Many species of birds, including wrens, swallows and tree-nesting ducks, will readily accept an appropriate man-made birdhouse as a place to raise a family. See the references listed on p. 89 for tips on building birdhouses. Feeders and birdhouses are also available commercially.

## Gardening to Attract Birds

Several trees, shrubs, herbs and other native plants attract many species of birds and satisfy some of their seasonal needs. Plants can provide seeds, berries and nectar, as well as nesting sites and/or materials.

In the Pacific Northwest, several native wildflowers, such as columbine (*Aquilegia* spp.) and penstemon (*Penstemon* spp.), are favorites of hummingbirds. Native plants that attract seed- and fruit-eating birds include maple (*Acer* spp.), arbutus (*Arbutus menziesii*), birch (*Betula* spp.), dogwood (*Cornus* spp.), hawthorn (*Crataegus* spp.), chokecherry (*Prunus virginiana*), crabapple (*Pyrus* spp.) and oak (*Quercus* spp.). In addition, several non-native plants that attract birds are available at nurseries.

However, please note that some plants, such as bracted honeysuckle (*Lonicera involucrata*), produce berries that are **poisonous to humans**, and are best avoided if they would be within reach of small children.

# Common Loon *Gavia immer*

DESCRIPTION **Summer:** Head black; neck black with a striped white necklace; back black with rows of white spots. **Winter:** Crown and nape dark gray; throat white with a faint white neck-band fading toward the back.
SIZE Length to 32" (80 cm).
NESTING **Nest:** At water's edge, made from various quatic plants piled in the water. **Eggs:** Normally 2, olive spotted with brown.
HABITAT Breeds on fresh water lakes and migrates to the ocean and along the coastline.

*Summer.*

*Winter.*

The distinctive mournful call of the common loon is often heard near lakes, where it breeds, and occasionally along the coast during its annual migration. The common loon population has been reduced, especially in the southern portion of its range. This species migrates along the Pacific coast and inland as it makes its way to and from its breeding grounds, as far north as Alaska. Loons dive to a depth of 264' (80 m) and have been clocked at speeds of 75 mph (120 km/h) while flying on migration.

**Similar Species:** The Pacific loon (*Gavia pacifica*), with its gray head and purple neck patch in breeding birds, is a similar species that may be observed while on migration. The similar red-throated loon (*Gavia stellata*) displays a gray head and red neck patch in its breeding plumage. As well, the squarish head of the common loon is noticeably different from the more rounded head of both the Pacific and red-throated loons.

# Pied-billed Grebe *Podilymbus podiceps*

**DESCRIPTION** Overall chicken-like body shape with short bill. **Summer:** Brown; throat patch black; eyes dark, each with a white eye-ring; bill short and white with a dark black ring. **Winter:** Black ring on bill very faint or non-existent. **SIZE** Length to 13 ½" (34 cm). **NESTING Nest:** Attached to live aquatic plants, near surface of water; made from decaying vegetation. **Eggs:** Normally 4–7, bluish green. **HABITAT** Year-round in ponds, lakes and marshes.

The pied-billed grebe is a solitary and secretive species that is famous for its wide array of vocalizations during breeding season in spring. Included in its repertoire is a loud and distinctive *kuk-kuk-kuk cow cow cow cowp cowp cowp*, along with various cooing noises and a gobbling call. It is a small grebe, and amazing in its ability to sink slowly into the water, submerging itself completely or up to its neck.

**Similar Species:** The horned grebe (*Podiceps auritus*) is often observed along the coast in winter and summer. During winter its crown and upper plumage are dark, while its underparts are white. In summer, it has a distinctive reddish neck and yellow "horns."

# Red-necked Grebe *Podiceps grisegena*

**DESCRIPTION Breeding adult:** Throat and cheeks white; foreneck reddish. **Winter:** Throat and foreneck dusky; chinstrap white. **SIZE** Length to 20" (50 cm). **NESTING Nest:** Floating nest, made from fresh and decayed vegetation and attached to live plants; solitary or in colonies. **Eggs:** Normally 4–5, bluish white. **HABITAT** Shallow lakes and wetlands during breeding season; along the coast during spring and fall migrations.

As in all grebes, the legs of the red-necked grebe are positioned far back on the body. This placement is excellent for swimming, but in order to fly, the bird requires a stretch of open water approximately 165' (50 m) long for takeoff. This limits the areas where the species can nest. The red-necked grebe nests alone or in loose colonies in shallow lakes and similar areas. Courtship practices include the male presenting aquatic vegetation to the female. When the young are still very small, they may be observed catching a ride on a parent's back. Common loons (p. 14) have been known to harass red-necked grebes at both nesting and hunting areas.

# Western Grebe *Aechmophorus occidentalis*

**DESCRIPTION** Overall black upper parts and white lower parts; head with distinctive black cap; neck long and narrow.
**SIZE** Length to 25" (63 cm).
**NESTING Nest:** Floating nest, made from fresh and decayed vegetation and attached to live plants; in colonies. **Eggs:** Normally 2–4, pale bluish white.
**HABITAT** Breeds on large lakes, and winters along the Pacific coast.

The western grebe uses its long bill to spear fish, the mainstay of its diet. It is normally a gregarious bird, nesting in groups with up to 90 pairs in a colony. The courtship display is truly spectacular—the birds perform their water ballet by skittering upright along the surface of the water. The ritual is enacted by a mated pair of birds, or two males, or (occasionally) one female accompanied by two males.

During the winter months, this species has often been observed on the coast in flocks numbering into the thousands. But populations have declined alarmingly in recent years because of disturbances in nesting areas.

# Pelagic Cormorant *Phalacrocorax pelagicus*

**DESCRIPTION Adult:** Black overall; white patches on flanks. **Breeding adult:** Crown and nape with tufts.
**SIZE** Length to 26" (65 cm).
**NESTING Nest:** On a cliff; in colonies. Nest materials include seaweed, grass, moss and sticks. **Eggs:** Normally 3–5, bluish white.
**HABITAT** Coastal waters.

The pelagic cormorant is the smallest and sleekest of our 3 western cormorant species. An expert fisher, like other ocean-going birds, it removes excess salt from its body through salt glands and excretes the salts in a concentrated solution. It also regurgitates pellets containing the indigestible parts of its prey, much as owls do.

**Similar Species:** Brandt's cormorant (*Phalacrocorax penicillatus*) is a similar species, but has a blue and yellow throat, and it seeks out rapidly moving waters. (Pelagic and double-crested cormorants prefer quieter areas.) The double-crested cormorant (*Phalacrocorax auritus*), which may also be seen on inland waters, has a yellow-orange throat pouch and is the only West Coast cormorant to fly with a kinked neck.

# Great Blue Heron *Ardea herodias*

**DESCRIPTION** Back and wings blue-gray; head white with black bar above eye; legs and neck very long.
**SIZE** Length to 46" (115 cm).
**NESTING Nest:** In a tree, made from sticks; in colonies. Normally to 20–60' (6–18 m) off the ground, occasionally more than 100' (30 m) up. **Eggs:** Normally 3–5, pale blue.
**HABITAT** Fresh water and salt water shorelines.

The great blue heron, a striking bird, is commonly seen throughout the Pacific Northwest. It is an expert fisher that is often observed standing in shallow water, patiently waiting for the right moment to strike. This heron feeds on fish, but also on frogs, salamanders, shrews and voles. If disturbed at a fishing site, it creates a great commotion, uttering a series of prehistoric-sounding shrieks—seemingly in anger at the intruder—before flying off.

Herons' courtship rituals include elaborate displays and presentations of sticks. Their colonies are easily disturbed and should not be approached, because great blue herons abandons their nests with little provocation. As well, bald eagles (p. 33) prey upon heron chicks in the nest.

# Trumpeter Swan *Cygnus buccinator*

**DESCRIPTION Adult:** White overall; neck elongated; bill and forehead form a straight ridge; bill black. **Juvenile:** Gray overall; bill pinkish with black tip.
**SIZE** Length to 60" (150 cm).
**NESTING Nest:** At water's edge, or built up in shallow water. **Eggs:** Normally 5–7, pale green.
**HABITAT** Fresh water and salt water shorelines.

The experience of observing trumpeter swans flying close by in a foggy mist, is truly memorable. This is an impressive swan and a commonly seen migrant in the Pacific Northwest in early spring, on its way to northern British Columbia and Alaska. As well, many individuals winter along the coast south to Oregon. The trumpeter swan is named for its deep, dis-

*Juvenile .*

tinctive, resonant voice, somewhat like the sound of a French horn. It is the largest of all North American waterfowl and requires a stretch of water 20' (6 m) long to become airborne.

Unfortunately its numbers have been reduced considerably from historic highs in North America during the 19th century, but today populations are increasing once again, thanks to human efforts to protect them.

*Adult trumpeter swan.*

**Similar Species:** The tundra swan (*Cygnus columbianus*) is a very similar swan that also migrates through the area while on its way to the Arctic. Its bill has a yellow patch of skin, and its voice resembles the sound produced by reed instruments. The mute swan (*Cygnus olor*) is an introduced species from Europe, often seen in urban parks. This species has an orange bill.

# Greater White-fronted Goose *Anser albifrons*

**DESCRIPTION** Dark head; belly light with dark speckles; bill pink or orange with white band around it.
**SIZE** Length to 28" (70 cm).
**NESTING Nest:** On ground near water, made from plant material, lined with down. **Eggs:** Normally 3–6, white.
**HABITAT** Wetlands and grassy areas as staging areas.

White-fronts are common migrants to and from their northern breeding grounds in Alaska and the western Arctic. This species is more commonly seen in autumn, while migrating south in small groups, but large flocks numbering into the thousands have also been observed. Hunters, and occasionally birders, often refer to this species as "speckle-belly." It is a large goose that feeds on grain, grass and the first lush new growth to follow a burn. Its voice while flying resembles laughter, with a distinctive *kah-lah-aluck*.

# Snow Goose *Chen caerulescens*

**DESCRIPTION** White overall; neck slender, wings with black tips.
**SIZE** Length to 28" (70 cm).
**NESTING Nest:** On a ridge or hummock; in colonies. **Eggs:** Normally 3–5, whitish.
**HABITAT** Various coastal and interior areas on migration.

Fall brings skeins or flocks of snow geese to the coastal regions of the Pacific Northwest. These annual migrations are an impressive sight, accompanied by an equally impressive noisy, excited clamor. Thousands of snow geese stay along the coast at their feeding areas until late March, when they begin migrating to their breeding grounds on Wrangel Island in northeast Siberia. Snows are known to cruise to altitudes as great as 6,000' (1,800 m) while on migration. There are two color phases of this species: white and blue (rarely observed in the Pacific Northwest). The total population has increased dramatically in recent years.

# Brant *Branta bernicla*

**DESCRIPTION** Black overall; hind end white. **SIZE** Length to 25" (63 cm). **NESTING Nest:** On the ground, made of grasses. **Eggs:** Normally 3–5, creamy white. **HABITAT** Along coastal bays and estuaries.

Migrating along the coast in March and April, this salt water goose makes its way north to breed in the tundra. Its feeding activities are regulated by the movements of the tides. The brant is well known for dining at "salad bars" of sea lettuce and eel-grass. It is an omnivore that also feeds on mollusks, worms and crustaceans. Migrating flocks do not form the "V" shape common in other geese. Instead they fly in undulating lateral strings of birds, seemingly without a leader. Fall migration is faster than spring, with both groups and scattered individuals moving through the area.

# Canada Goose *Branta canadensis*

**DESCRIPTION** Back and wings brown; head and neck black with a distinctive white chinstrap. **SIZE** Length to 45" (114 cm). **NESTING Nest:** On the ground near water, in a tree, up to 102' (31 m) off the ground, or at the edge of a cliff. Nest is made of sticks, grass and moss, and lined with down. **Eggs:** Normally 4–7, white. **HABITAT** Fresh water or salt water areas.

The Canada goose is a common year-round resident over much of North America. Its numbers have increased steadily, largely because of the work of biologists and the availability of large new feeding areas such as golf courses. Today their nests can also be found within the boundaries of many cities. Canada geese mate for life and are known to live as long as 30 years. They usually feed on a variety of vegetation, and young geese gain weight rapidly and fledge in 63 days. Their migration is characterized by flying "V" formations.

# Wood Duck *Aix sponsa*

**DESCRIPTION Breeding male:** Head iridescent green with flattened crest; breast reddish brown. **Female:** Much more subdued in color; head with a white eye ring.
**SIZE** Length to 18" (45 cm).
**NESTING Nest:** In a large tree cavity or nest box close to water, up to 65' (20 m) off the ground. **Eggs:** Normally 9–14, white to buff.
**HABITAT** Near lakes surrounded by deciduous woodland.

When it comes to color, few birds rival the striking male wood duck, a spectacular species that is named for its habitat of wooded areas. This duck is also well known for its ability to fly through woodlands by twisting and dodging, without losing a beat. When young ducks hatch, they leap to the ground and make their way to the water. In many areas of this species' range, tree cavities are uncommon, so nest boxes are built to attract nesting pairs. These boxes have proven successful in dramatically increasing populations.

# Green-winged Teal *Anas crecca*

**DESCRIPTION Breeding male:** Gray overall; head cinnamon with an iridescent green ear patch. **Female:** Brown overall. **Adult:** Speculum green.
**SIZE** Length to 14 ½" (36 cm).
**NESTING Nest:** On the ground, made of grasses, weeds and twigs, and lined with down. **Eggs:** Normally 6–11, cream to buff.
**HABITAT** Fresh water and salt water areas.

This common species, well known for its swift flight, is a small duck, often found in small flocks. It is known to live as long as 16 years, although the average lifespan is probably shorter.
Nests are located in woodland areas near wetlands. The male's voice is a distinctive high-pitched whistle, while the female's is reminiscent of the mallard's quack.

# Mallard *Anas platyrhynchos*

**DESCRIPTION Adult:**
Speculum or wing patch
bright blue with white edges;
legs and feet bright orange.
**Breeding male:** Head iridescent green.
**SIZE** Length to 23" (58 cm).
**NESTING Nest:** Normally on
the ground, made of reeds or
grasses, and lined with down.
**Eggs:** Normally 7–10, occasionally to 15, olive.
**HABITAT** Marshes, ponds,
bogs, lakes and similar situations.

*Female.*

*Drake.*

The mallard is likely the most common species of waterfowl in North America and perhaps in
the entire north temperate zone. Its presence is often announced by the loud *quack, quack,
quack* of the female. These ducks dine on a wide variety of foods, including aquatic vegetation, seeds and aquatic insects, and they are well known, especially by hunters, for their love
of grain and corn. The mallard is a familiar sight in urban parks throughout much of North
America. It is important not to feed bread to this species or any wild bird, because it has no
nutritional value for birds (see p. 12).

# Northern Pintail *Anas acuta*

**DESCRIPTION Breeding male:** Head chocolate brown; body gray; breast white; tail elongated. **Female:** Overall brown; tail pointed.
**SIZE** Length to 26" (65 cm).
**NESTING Nest:** On the ground, made of grasses and leaves, and lined with down. **Eggs:** Normally 6–10, pale olive.
**HABITAT** Wetlands.

It is reported that more than a million northern pintails migrate along the Pacific coast to the breeding areas of Alaska. Like mallards (see opposite), these birds migrate in large flocks.

In the northern pintail, as in many birds, females are often subtle in coloration while their mates are brightly colored. This difference is believed to aid in the survival of a species. Females normally incubate the eggs, and their subdued coloration helps prevent them from being detected by predators. The bright colors of males, on the other hand, draw attention away from the female and the nest site.

# Blue-winged Teal *Anas discors*

**DESCRIPTION Breeding male:** Head bluish gray with white crescent; wing with large blue patch and green speculum. **Female:** Brown overall; wing with large blue patch and green speculum.
**SIZE** Length to 16" (40 cm).
**NESTING Nest:** On the ground in open areas, made of grasses and weeds lining a depression. **Eggs:** Normally 9–13, white to olive.
**HABITAT** Ponds and marshes.

The blue-winged teal is a rapid flier with expert aviation skills, twisting and turning with fine precision in small groups. This species rarely tips up. It feeds primarily on the water surface and occasionally on the shoreline, eating mainly seeds as well as vegetative portions of aquatic plants. The blue-winged teal migrates north in late spring, and shortens its northern stay even further by returning early in the fall. Ring-necked pheasants (p. 38) have been known occasionally to lay their eggs in the nests of the blue-winged teal.

# Northern Shoveler *Anas clypeata*

**DESCRIPTION Breeding male:** White overall; head iridescent green; body with orange patches on sides; bill large and spoon-shaped. **Female:** Brown overall; bill large and spoon-shaped.
**SIZE** Length to 19" (48 cm).
**NESTING Nest:** On the ground, near water, made of dried grasses and weeds, and lined with down. **Eggs:** Normally 9–12, pale olive.
**HABITAT** Marshes, ponds, bogs, lakes and similar situations.

This common puddle duck is often seen in small groups, during migration to and from the nesting areas. Courtship rituals begin with the male uttering a guttural *konk, konk, konk* while repeatedly craning his neck and raising his head. If the female approves, the two birds swim in circles, one behind the other, with water running through their bills. Eventually the female lays her eggs in a ground nest. During migration, these ducks may be observed in larger numbers feeding together in various wetlands.

# Gadwall *Anas strepera*

**DESCRIPTION Breeding male:** Gray overall; belly white; rump black; wing patch white. **Female:** Overall a mixture of browns; belly white; wing patch white.
**SIZE** Length to 20" (50 cm).
**NESTING Nest:** On the ground, often near water, made of dried grasses and weeds, and lined with down. **Eggs:** Normally 8–10, white. Some nests contain the eggs of 2 or more females.
**HABITAT** Wetlands.

The gadwall often goes unnoticed because of its dull coloration, but the colors are distinctive upon close examination. The female gadwall is especially impressed with the male's speculum and black color. Gadwalls are dabblers that favor small wetlands as their resorts and breeding areas. Most are year-round residents, but many individuals migrate through the area on their way to northern breeding areas. Some long-distance migrants have been known to travel as far as 1,500 miles (2,500 km) to reach their southern destination.

# Eurasian Wigeon *Anas penelope*

**DESCRIPTION Breeding male:** Gray overall; head reddish brown with a cream-colored forehead. **Female:** Reddish overall.
**SIZE** Length to 20" (50 cm).
**NESTING Nest:** On the ground, usually near water. Nest materials include dried grasses; nest is lined with down. **Eggs:** Normally 8–9, whitish.
**HABITAT** Fresh water and salt water areas.

Eurasian wigeons are often observed individually or in small numbers, mixed in with large flocks of the American wigeon (see below). In fact, these visitors are one of the treasures that birders look for among American wigeon. A winter migrant that originated in Siberia and western Alaska, the Eurasian wigeon is rarely seen here during the summer months. Males are seen more often than females, because females are very similar to female American wigeons and often go unnoticed.

---

# American Wigeon *Anas americana*

**DESCRIPTION Breeding male:** Gray head with a white cap and green ear patch. **Female:** Brown overall; head gray; belly white. **Adult:** White wing patch.
**SIZE** Length to 19" (48 cm).
**NESTING Nest:** On the ground, made of dried grasses and weeds, and lined with down. **Eggs:** Normally 8–11, whitish.
**HABITAT** Areas near fresh water and salt water.

The American wigeon, a common year-round resident of the coast, feeds primarily on vegetation, especially pond weeds, grasses, algae and sedges. Large flocks are often found wintering in areas that have big grassy areas, such as golf courses. American wigeons are also known to help themselves to the food items accidentally dropped by diving water birds, including the canvasback (p. 26) and American coot (p. 42). The American wigeon was once called the baldpate because of the white or "bald" spot on the head.

# Canvasback *Aythya valisineria*

**DESCRIPTION Male:** Body white; head red; forehead slopes smoothly into the long bill. **Female:** Body gray; head brownish.
**SIZE** Length to 21" (53 cm).
**NESTING Nest:** Large and basket-like, in marsh vegetation above water or on dry ground. Nest materials include a wide variety of dead plants. **Eggs:** Normally 7–12, olive.
**HABITAT** Fresh water areas with abundant vegetation along the edge.

Canvasbacks feed by diving for the succulent roots of various plants found at their "lake resort." They also feed on fishes, tadpoles, leeches, snails and mollusks. This is a diving duck that migrates along the coast and nests at inland sites.

**Similar Species:** Occasionally a female places one or more eggs in the nest of another pair or even another species. The redhead (*Aythya americana*), a similar looking species with a rounded red head, is known to leave eggs in the nests of canvasbacks. This is probably a survival mechanism. It is safer to let another female incubate one or more of your eggs, in case a predator finds your nest—in other words, not to place all your eggs in one basket.

# Ring-necked Duck *Aythya collaris*

**DESCRIPTION Male:** Back dark; chest black; head purple, often appearing black. **Female:** Dark brown, white eye ring.
**SIZE** Length to 18" (45 cm).
**NESTING Nest:** On the ground or on floating vegetation. Nest materials include grass, sedges and weeds; nest is lined with down. **Eggs:** Normally 8–10, olive to buff.
**HABITAT** Fresh water marshes.

The ring-necked duck is a year-round resident that looks very similar to the lesser scaup (p. 27), which it often accompanies. This omnivore feeds on grain, pond weeds, water lily bulbs, frogs, crawfish, insects and snails.

Individuals gather into flocks by early May to migrate to their breeding grounds inland. Many individuals remain near the coast through the winter months. The ring on this species is so difficult to see that perhaps it should be called ring-billed duck.

# Greater Scaup *Aythya marila*

**DESCRIPTION** **Breeding male:** Back gray; chest black; head greenish and glossy. The head is smooth and rounded. **Female:** Brown overall; head dark with a white patch adjacent to the bill and a crescent-shaped spot behind the ear.
**SIZE** Length to 18" (45 cm).
**NESTING** **Nest:** On the ground, often on an island; in loose colonies. Nest is made from dead plants. **Eggs:** Normally 7–9, olive-buff.
**HABITAT** Primarily salt water and large fresh water bodies.

The greater scaup is a common species that winters and migrates along the coast. It is also found inland on a variety of wetlands, but in reduced numbers. It is an agile diver that can spend up to 60 seconds underwater. Greater scaups nest in Alaska and Yukon.

**Similar Species:** The greater and lesser scaup (see below) are quite similar in appearance and are often mistaken for each other. Head coloration usually differs but it is not a reliable distinguishing characteristic. The greater scaup is slightly larger, and its head is round compared to the more triangular head of the lesser scaup.

# Lesser Scaup *Aythya affinis*

**DESCRIPTION** **Breeding male:** Back gray; chest black; head purple (may also show some green). Head is triangular in shape with a peaked crown. **Female:** Brown overall; head with a white patch adjacent to the bill.
**SIZE** Length to 16 ½" (41 cm).
**NESTING** **Nest:** On the ground, often on a fresh-water island, made from dry grass, lined with down. **Eggs:** Normally 9–11, olive-buff.
**HABITAT** Primarily near smaller bodies of fresh water deep enough for diving ducks.

The lesser scaup is a year-round resident that is more common inland than its close relative, the greater scaup (see above). It is a common duck that nests on islands when they are available. Meal selections include such gourmet items as mollusks, worms, fry, crawfish, water insects and larvae. The flight of the lesser scaup is well known for its erratic pattern, with much twisting and turning.

# Harlequin Duck *Histrionicus histrionicus*

**DESCRIPTION Breeding male:** Striking harlequin-like colors. **Female:** Brown overall; head with three white areas.
**SIZE** Length to 16 ½" (41 cm).
**NESTING Nest:** On the ground, often near water, made of grasses and twigs, lined with down. **Eggs:** Normally 5–7, pale buff.
**HABITAT** Along the coast and mountain streams.

Harlequin ducks bounce around like corks in the water. For breeding, they favor areas with the roughest of mountain streams. They sometimes get broken bones while being tossed about, but the bones usually mend. Males accompany females to the breeding grounds but do not assist in raising young; instead they return to the coast. The females return to the coast later with that year's young.

The diet of harlequins changes with the seasons. While on the breeding grounds, they feed on aquatic invertebrates such as the larvae of stoneflies, midges and others. Like American dippers (p. 72), they can walk along the bottoms of streams, feeding underwater for up to half a minute. On the coast, however, they feed on other invertebrates, including snails, small crabs, mussels and fish. In some areas, boating activity on sensitive breeding streams interferes with reproduction and feeding.

# Surf Scoter *Melanitta perspicillata*

**DESCRIPTION Male:** Black overall; head with white patches on forehead and back of head; bill large with orange coloration. **Female:** Brown overall; head with white patches on side of face.
**SIZE** Length to 21" (53 cm).
**NESTING Nest:** On the ground. Nest is made in a depression and lined with down. **Eggs:** Normally 5–9, buff.
**HABITAT** Salt water and fresh water areas.

The surf scoter is a sea duck that is commonly seen in large flotillas along the coast, sometimes numbering into the thousands. Like other scoters, this one needs a strong wind in order to take off from the water and fly. In late spring, these birds leave the coastline to fly north and breed. Their diet on the coast consists of mollusks, crustaceans and fish.

**Similar Species:** The white-winged scoter (*Melanitta fusca*) is similar in appearance, but it displays a prominent white patch on its wings and lacks the bright orange bill and white patches on the head.

# Common Goldeneye *Bucephala clangula*

**DESCRIPTION Breeding male:** Back and wings black barred with white; breast white; head dark with greenish sheen and a round white spot on the cheek; eyes golden. **Female:** Brown overall; head dark brown.
**SIZE** Length to 20" (50 cm).
**NESTING Nest:** In a tree cavity, 5–60' (1.5–18 m) off the ground.
**Eggs:** Normally 7–10, olive green.
**HABITAT** Fresh water and salt water areas.

Both common and Barrow's goldeneyes (see below) are well known for their swift flight and the whistling sound of the air rushing through their wings. Spring courtship rituals include an elaborate head-bobbing display by the male. Females are known for their determination to find nesting spots—some have even been known to make their way down chimneys in the search. When nature's accommodation is at a premium, they use nest boxes where available, and two females may deposit their eggs in the same nest.

# Barrow's Goldeneye *Bucephala islandica*

**DESCRIPTION Breeding male:** Back and wings black barred with white; head dark with a purple sheen and a crescent-shaped spot on the cheek. **Female:** Brown overall.
**SIZE** Length to 20" (50 cm).
**NESTING Nest:** In a tree cavity, rock crevice or nest box. **Eggs:** Normally 7–10, olive green.
**HABITAT** Fresh water and salt water areas.

Barrow's goldeneyes nest inland and winter along the coast. Like common goldeneyes (see above), which are close relatives, Barrow's goldeneyes are cavity nesters. The newly hatched young tumble out of the nest and bounce unharmed onto the ground, and the female then leads them to water and watches over them for approximately 56 days. On the coast, this diving duck feasts on a wide variety of delicacies such as mussels, clams, snails and barnacles, which are often found by turning up pebbles in shallow water.

# Bufflehead *Bucephala albeola*

**DESCRIPTION Breeding male:** Back black; lower body white; head iridescent green with a hint of purple and a white patch on the crown. **Female:** Light brown overall; head dark brown with a white spot. **SIZE** Length to 13 ½" (34 cm). **NESTING Nest:** In a tree cavity, 2–50' (.6–15 m) off the ground. **Eggs:** Normally 8–10, cream colored. **HABITAT** Fresh water and salt water areas.

This common species, which gets its name from the puffy appearance of its head, is conspicuously small and never found in large numbers. It commonly migrates along the coast where many individuals winter as well. Pairs of buffleheads remain together for a considerable time and repeatedly return to the same nesting area, near water but away from the coast, where they use the abandoned nests of northern flickers (p. 64). Their diet is varied and includes both fish and fish eggs. The bufflehead has been known to live as long as 13 years.

# Hooded Merganser *Lophodytes cucullatus*

**DESCRIPTION Male:** Head black; crest features a large white patch; back black. **Female:** Body brown; head with a light brown crest. **SIZE** Length to 18" (45 cm). **NESTING Nest:** In a large tree cavity close to water, 10–80' (3–24 m) off the ground. **Eggs:** Normally 10–12; occasionally to 18, white. **HABITAT** Woodland ponds and rivers.

*Male with raised crest.*

The impressive spectacle of the male hooded merganser's crest, raised during courtship, is one of the highlights of spring. (At other times, the crest lies flat on the drake's head.) During the summer months, this bird gathers in smaller numbers, while in the fall, larger groups may congregate. The female carries her young by the neck from the nesting cavity to the water. This species is also one of the fastest of ducks, with a speed that approaches the "velocity of a bullet," as one observer noted. Hooded mergansers can be found from sea level to elevations of 4,800' (1,440 m).

# Red-breasted Merganser *Mergus serrator*

DESCRIPTION **Breeding male:** Head dark green with a shaggy crest; neck with a white ring; breast rusty. **Female:** Head brown, fading to white breast.
SIZE Length to 23" (58 cm).
NESTING **Nest:** Usually on the ground, but also in hollow stumps or burrows. The nest is a slight depression or hollow, lined with down. **Eggs:** Normally 7–10, olive buff.
HABITAT Lakes, rivers and coastal bays.

The springtime antics of mergansers are a treat to observe. The elaborate courtship display of the red-breasted merganser begins with the male reaching forward with his neck and raising it so that he can abruptly dunk the front portion of his body underwater while keeping his head above the surface. He then opens his bright red bill and pivots his body in a stiff manner. If several suitors are present to compete, the performance is especially spectacular. Eventually the female chooses a single male, and lays her eggs and incubates them herself. She is responsible for raising the young; as many as 100 young from several broods may be watched over by a single female.

# Common Merganser *Mergus merganser*

DESCRIPTION **Male:** Head green and lacking a crest; breast white. **Female:** Light brown overall; head rust colored with a crest; breast white; distinct border between rust-colored neck and white breast.
SIZE Length to 25" (63 cm).
NESTING **Nest:** Usually near water, in a large tree cavity or rock crevice, or under a tree bank. **Eggs:** Normally 8–11, buff.
HABITAT Fresh water and salt water areas.

Like others in the merganser clan, the common merganser is primarily a fish eater. The toothed bill enables this bird to capture the slipperiest of fish. Flocks of common mergansers are known to work collectively to drive fish into a bay and feast on their prize. They also feed on mussels and various other mollusks. The young of this year-round resident eat heartily, up to an impressive 80% of their body weight per day when they are only 10 days old.

# Turkey Vulture *Cathartes aura*

**DESCRIPTION Adult:** Brownish black overall; head small, red and unfeathered compared to the bald eagle (see opposite). **Juvenile:** Head black.
**SIZE** Length to 32" (80 cm).
**NESTING Nest:** In a sheltered location such as a cliff, cave or dense thicket. **Eggs:** Normally 2, placed on ground or on debris, whitish with brown and lavender blotches.
**HABITAT** Primarily observed in flight, or while roosting on open snags.

It is truly amazing to watch turkey vultures as they soar, apparently effortlessly, without so much as a single wing beat. With their V-shaped wings, these masters of the air often ride thermals in the company of bald eagles. They are summer residents, present only during the warmer months of summer as far north as southern British Columbia. By September, however, turkey vultures begin to migrate south, moving along the coast to their wintering grounds from California to South America.

This bird has a highly developed sense of smell, with which it finds carrion, its main food item. Turkey vultures perform an important duty as sanitation engineers. They also have an amazing ability to tolerate botulism—an essential feature if you feed on carrion. These birds spend a large part of their days roosting in snags at higher elevations.

# Osprey *Pandion haliaetus*

**DESCRIPTION** Adult chocolate brown above; white below; wings long and angled backward at the bend; dark line from eye to neck; distinctive black "wrists" visible from below when the bird is in flight.
**SIZE** Length to 25" (63 cm).
**NESTING Nest:** On top of a tree or snag. Nest is a platform made from sticks. **Eggs:** Normally 3, cream colored with brown blotches.
**HABITAT** Near the ocean or lakes with fish.

The osprey is a world citizen, truly cosmo-politan in both temperate and tropical areas of the globe. With its dramatic wingspan to 6' (1.8 m), the bird hovers above the water while hunting for fish. It is well known for its spectacular dives, often emerging from the water with an impressive fish that even a human would be proud of catching, although some fish are lost to raiding bald eagles (see opposite).

The osprey is well equipped to survive with many useful adaptations. Its oily feathers effectively repel water even after repeated dives. The angular shape of the wings ensures that they are not injured when the bird dives into the water at high speed. The talons are more curved than those of other birds of prey and are enhanced by spiny spicules with which the osprey can grasp slippery fish.

# Bald Eagle *Haliaeetus leucocephalus*

**DESCRIPTION Adult:** Dark brown overall; head white; tail white. **Juvenile:** Overall dark brown; white feathers appear on the head in the fourth year and proportion of white feathers on the head increases with age.
**SIZE** Length 31–37" (78–93 cm).
**NESTING Nest:** On a cliff or in a tree, to 180' (54 m) or more off the ground. Nest is an accumulation of sticks that is added to over the years. **Eggs:** Normally 2, white.
**HABITAT** Along the coast and near large lakes containing fish.

The bald eagle is a grand species that always commands attention, whether it is sitting in a tree or soaring high in the sky. In autumn, large numbers of this scavenger are attracted to spawning salmon streams. Here, spent salmon provide food for both the adult eagles and inexperienced young. However, the bald eagle is also a skillful predator, hunting fish, waterfowl and other birds on the water and remaining ever watchful for the right moment to claim its prize. And it is adept at harassing the osprey (see opposite), causing it to drop its fish; occasionally the eagle will catch the fish at lightning speed before it touches the water. Like the turkey vulture (opposite), this large bird of prey can also use thermals to circle at amazing heights.

*Adult.*

*Juvenile.*

# Sharp-shinned Hawk *Accipiter striatus*

**DESCRIPTION Male:** Dark blue above; barred breast; wings rounded; tail long, barred and noticeably squared off. **Female:** Dark brown above.
**SIZE** Length 9–13" (23–33 cm).
**NESTING Nest:** Usually in a conifer, 20–60' (6–18 m) off the ground. Nest is made from sticks and lined with strips of bark. **Eggs:** Normally 4–5, white with brown blotches.
**HABITAT** Forested areas and woodlands.

Fear reigns among many forest birds when this little resident predator is nearby. The sharp-shinned hawk sits quietly on a perch in a wooded area, waiting for its prey and then chasing small birds, dodging branches as it goes. The similar-sized merlin (see p. 37) does not actively hunt by chasing its prey through trees. Females are much larger and weigh almost twice as much as males. Their prey also differs significantly: females tend to take birds the size of grosbeaks, while males are often successful with junco-sized birds.

**Similar Species:** Identification of the sharp-shinned hawk and several similar species can be difficult. Key features to look for include overall size, as well as shape of wings and tail.

# Cooper's Hawk *Accipiter cooperii*

**DESCRIPTION** Similar to sharp-shinned hawk (see above) but larger; slate-gray above; tail longer, barred and rounded; head with black cap.
**SIZE** Length 14–19" (35–48cm).
**NESTING Nest:** In a tree, 25–50' (7–15 m) off the ground, made from sticks and lined with bark strips. **Eggs:** Normally 3–5, bluish white with dark markings.
**HABITAT** Forested areas and woodlands.

Closely related to the sharp-shinned hawk (see above), the Cooper's hawk is larger overall with a longer tail. This hawk feeds primarily on birds as big as ducks, and some small mammals. It is often seen sitting out in the open, waiting to attack its prey rather than chasing it.

Cooper's hawks were once among the most common hawks in North America, and as year-round residents, some coastal populations reach the highest concentrations to be found anywhere on the continent. But its numbers are declining. Some biologists believe that the reduction in populations of small birds may be the prime cause.

# Northern Goshawk *Accipiter gentilis*

**DESCRIPTION Adult:** Dark gray above; light gray below; cap dark; eyebrow white. **SIZE** Length to 26" (65 cm). **NESTING Nest:** In a tree, usually 25–50' (7–15 m) off the ground. Nest materials include sticks of various sizes and green foliage. **Eggs:** Normally 2–4, bluish fading to white. **HABITAT** Coniferous and mixed-wood forests.

The northern goshawk is noted for vigorously defending its nest from a variety of enemies, including people—a confrontation that can draw blood. This powerful predator hunts inside the forest, often perching on branch until prey is spotted. At this point, the bird flies off to pursue the prey with a short burst of amazing speed, swerving to avoid branches and often crashing through thickets. At the nest, the female remains with the young while the male hunts and brings home the food. Populations of the northern goshawk are declining, probably because of loss of habitat.

# Red-tailed Hawk *Buteo jamaicensis*

**DESCRIPTION Adult:** Dark-brown above; upper surface of tail normally brick red; dark belt across the abdomen. **SIZE** Length to 24" (60 cm). **NESTING Nest:** In a tree, to 120' (36 m) off the ground, made from sticks and lined with fine materials. **Eggs:** Normally 2–3, white with brown blotches. **HABITAT** Forested areas.

The red-tailed hawk is a common and widespread bird of prey found throughout much of North America. Often observed sitting on a treetop or a telephone pole, this hawk is ever watchful for its next meal. Courtship rituals often include elaborate dives and other aerial acrobatics. The bird emits a distinctive harsh scream, sometimes transcribed as *keeeeer,* while it circles above the ground. Its diet includes mice, voles, ground squirrels, rabbits, small birds, garter snakes and occasionally insects. Like so many other raptors, this species was persecuted for years and now is protected, performing a valuable service by controlling rodents in agricultural areas. The red-tailed hawk is known to live as long as 16 years.

# Rough-legged Hawk Buteo lagopus

**DESCRIPTION** Overall mottled brown; tail white with one or more bands.
**SIZE** Length to 22" (55 cm).
**NESTING Nest:** Usually on a ledge. Nest materials include sticks, bones and debris; nest is lined with grasses and twigs. **Eggs:** Normally 3–5, bluish white with brown and violet blotches.
**HABITAT** Open areas while on migration.

Rough-legged hawks are commonly observed while away from their breeding areas across the North American tundra. This species winters from southern British Columbia to central California, so it is commonly seen in the Pacific Northwest between October and March. This is a large hawk, whose numbers fluctuate widely in response to changes in rodent populations. Occasionally it feeds on birds, amphibians and larger insects as well as rodents. To hunt, this hawk may hover over a potential meal or sit and wait on a perch, much like other species of hawks.

# Northern Harrier Circus cyaneus

**DESCRIPTION Male:** Gray-blue above; tail long; rump white; breast white and spotted. **Female:** Similar to male but with brown coloration. **Juvenile:** Similar to female but cinnamon below.
**SIZE** Length to 23" (58 cm).
**NESTING Nest:** Over shallow water or on the ground, in a field or marsh. Nest materials include sticks, grass and weeds. **Eggs:** Normally 4–6, bluish white, sometimes spotted with brown.
**HABITAT** Near wetlands.

Once called the marsh hawk, the northern harrier is a common inhabitant of the marsh. It carries out a seemingly endless search for food, travelling more than 60 miles (100 km) per day in search of food. Occasionally this raptor can be seen stalling in mid-flight when a slight movement is detected, then dropping into the grass to collect a treat such as a vole, young bird, frog or grasshopper. The northern harrier flies slowly and near the ground, except during the breeding display and while on migration. Males are well known for their swooping "sky-dancing" moves early in the breeding season, maneuvers that consist of vertical climbs and dives directed to prospective mates. Males are often polygamous, mating with as many as three females.

The northern harrier normally nests in wetlands, many of which are now being lost to development.

# Merlin *Falco columbarius*

**DESCRIPTION Male:** Light blue above; wings long and pointed; tail long with four black bars; breast streaked with brown. **Female:** Similar but brown overall; larger than male.
**SIZE** Length to 12" (30 cm).
**NESTING Nest:** In the abandoned nest of a hawk or crow, 10–60' (3–18 m) off the ground. No new nest materials are usually added. **Eggs:** Normally 4–5, whitish with reddish brown markings.
**HABITAT** Forested areas.

The merlin often occupies the abandoned nest of another species such as the American crow (p. 68), but it is very adaptable and may also take up residence on a cliff ledge or in a tree cavity. It is a falcon that normally hunts alone, but has been reported to hunt cooperatively with other merlins. In urban areas it frequently feeds on house sparrows (p. 87). It is reputed to be a belligerent raptor that will not tolerate other birds of prey in its vicinity.

The female merlin is larger than the male. Size is an important consideration to identify this species. Formerly called the pigeon hawk, this small falcon is quite vocal, often heard before it is seen with a high-pitched *ki ki ki ki ki ki ki*.

# Peregrine Falcon *Falco peregrinus*

**DESCRIPTION** Black to bluish above; barred below; wings slender; tail long; head with distinctive dark sideburns.
**SIZE** Length to 18" (45 cm).
**NESTING Nest:** On a cliff ledge or tall building. No nest is made. **Eggs:** Normally 3-4, reddish brown with dark brown blotches.
**HABITAT** Along rivers, large streams and marine shorelines.

The Peregrine falcon is often observed quietly sitting on a snag watching for an unwary duck or shorebird. It is the fastest bird in the world, capable of reaching estimated speeds of 200 mph (320 km/h) during a stoop (closed-wing dive). With this speed, the peregrine can kill its prey instantly in the sky, and it has also been reported to catch it in mid-air. The Peregrine rarely hunts birds that are sitting on the water; it waits until they take flight, when they are much more vulnerable.

This raptor nests early in the season. It selects a cliff ledge or similar spot, protected from the elements, to raise its young. In many cities today, with the help of humans, peregrines nest on high-rise buildings. Thanks to these protected nesting sites and a diet of rock doves (see p. 55), Peregrine falcon populations have increased. The Peregrine is known to live as long as 14 years.

# Ring-necked Pheasant *Phasianus colchicus*

**DESCRIPTION Breeding male:** Iridescent bronze body; head dark green with red comb and skin surrounding eye; tail very long and pointed.
**SIZE** Length to 33" (83 cm).
**NESTING Nest:** On the ground. Nest is a depression lined with grass and similar materials. **Eggs:** Normally 10–12, buff.
**HABITAT** Thickets next to agricultural crops.

In the springtime, the magnificent male ring-necked pheasant crows and beats his wings in order to advertise his presence to other males and his harem of females. During courtship, his comb becomes erect and the bare skin around his eye becomes vivid red. This year-round resident, an introduced species from China, has been brought to North American many times, for purposes of sport hunting. Numbers of the ring-necked pheasant are currently dwindling due to loss of habitat and predation by coyotes.

# Blue Grouse *Dendragapus obscurus*

**DESCRIPTION Breeding male:** Sooty gray; orange comb above eye; neck patch purple or yellow with a white edge. **Female:** Mottled brown.
**SIZE** Length to 20" (50 cm).
**NESTING Nest:** On the ground, under shelter such as a log or ledge. Nest materials include twigs, conifer needles and leaves. **Eggs:** Normally 5–10, buff with brown speckles.
**HABITAT** Various forested areas.

The blue grouse is a year-round resident of considerable size. The male produces a deep, resonant *hoot, hoot, hoot* as part of the breeding display. When his neck patch is inflated, the sound is amplified and can be heard at quite a distance. The male's display also includes raised eyebrows and a neck patch that becomes yellow (in birds along the coast) or vivid purple (in birds in the interior). This grouse has even been known to display toward a human being when the color of the person's clothes is similar to that of the male's neck patch. In some areas the blue grouse migrates uphill and downhill seasonally.

# White-tailed Ptarmigan *Lagopus leucurus*

**DESCRIPTION Summer:** Brown and white; eye comb red; tail white. **Winter:** Overall white, including tail.
**SIZE** Length to 12 ½" (31 cm).
**NESTING Nest:** On the ground, made from various plants and other materials, lined with feathers. **Eggs:** Normally 2–8, cinnamon with brown speckles.
**HABITAT** Mountainous regions.

The white-tailed ptarmigan, a member of the grouse clan, is a year-round resident of the mountains. It summers in alpine regions, and migrates over short distances and elevations to its winter range. Its coloration is a remarkably effective camouflage. This species can be found farther south than any other ptarmigan in North America. Buds form an important part of its winter diet.

*Spring molt plumage.*

Because ptarmigans live in cold, harsh environments, their toes are feathered to the tips to keep them warm in even the coldest weather.

*Summer plumage.*

39

# Ruffed Grouse *Bonasa umbellus*

**DESCRIPTION Adult:** Brown speckled with white and black; small crest. **Breeding male:** Neck with black ruff. **SIZE** Length to 17" (43 cm). **NESTING Nest:** On the ground, usually next to a log or at the base of a tree, made from leaves and grass, lined with feathers. **Eggs:** Normally 9–12, buff, occasionally with brown speckles. **HABITAT** Woodlands and forest regions.

The ruffed grouse is well known for its loud drumming in the springtime. As part of his breeding display, the male stands on a log with his ruffs extended, tail fanned and wings trailing. At irregular intervals, the bird beats his wings rapidly through the air to make a drumming sound. This display is a way of announcing his presence to other ruffed grouse in the area and claiming his territory.

*Male on drumming log.*

This year-round resident feeds on the buds, seeds and fruit of a wide range of plants. It is known all over the world for its 10-year cycle: over a 10-year period its population increases rapidly for several years, then plummets, and the cycle repeats. Increases in population are followed by increases in predator numbers, which then reduce the ruffed grouse population to very low numbers. These predators include the red-tailed hawk (see p. 35) and red fox.

*Nest and eggs.*

# California Quail *Callipepla californica*

**DESCRIPTION Adult:** Back and wings brown; chest blue-gray; one or two teardrop-shaped head plumes; chin patch black. **SIZE** Length to 10" (25 cm). **NESTING Nest:** On the ground, near a large rock or log. Nest is a depression lined with grass and dead leaves. **Eggs:** Normally 10–16, white. **HABITAT** A wide variety of open habitats.

The California quail is an active species, often seen scurrying across roads or open areas. It is a year-round resident that is common in California and has been successfully introduced to several areas in Washington and on Vancouver Island. This bird is known for laying its eggs in the nests of other species, including the ring-necked pheasant (see p. 38).

**Similar Species:** The similar mountain quail (*Oreortyx pictus*), sometimes encountered in the Pacific Northwest, has a reddish chin patch and a pair of thin head plumes.

# Virginia Rail *Rallus limicola*

**DESCRIPTION Adult:** Upper parts dark brown; cheeks gray; breast, foreneck and wings chestnut; bill and legs reddish. **Juvenile:** Darker overall. **SIZE** Length to 9 ½" (24 cm). **NESTING Nest:** In marsh areas, often near shallow water. Nest is a platform of cattails, reeds and grasses. **Eggs:** Normally 3–5, buff with brown and gray spots. **HABITAT** Fresh and brackish marshes.

The Virginia rail is a secretive species that is well known for a variety of calls. In fact, it is so secretive that it is heard more often than it is seen. Included in its repertoire is the frequently heard *kid kid kidick kidick*, as well as a distinctive series of *oink* calls in decreasing volume. Those who are lucky enough to observe this species will see that its long toes are very effective in keeping it on top of the mud, where it often walks. This rail's diet includes a wide variety of invertebrates, including insects, snails and earthworms, as well as a wide variety of aquatic insect larvae.

# American Coot *Fulica americana*

DESCRIPTION **Adult:** Black overall; bill whitish; legs and feet from yellow to orange. **Juvenile:** Legs and feet greenish.
SIZE Length to 15 ½" (39 cm).
NESTING **Nest:** Floating nest, made of dead vegetation. **Eggs:** Normally 6–11, buff with brownish spots.
HABITAT Fresh water marshes, ponds and sloughs.

The American coot is a member of the rail family but resembles a duck. It is a year-round resident with breeding pairs found throughout the Pacific Northwest. Many other individuals migrate in spring from southern climates, including California and Mexico. This bird often forms large flocks during migration.

In the springtime, downy young coots are sometimes observed, but they look so different that the observer cannot always determine what species they are. Their colorful bristle-like orange down does not resemble the plumage of an adult. Eventually these downy young molt, and begin to resemble adults.

A whitish shield extends from the bill to the forehead. This shield varies greatly in shape from one individual to another and grows larger during the breeding season. The size and shape of the shield seem to play an important part in birds recognizing each other.

# Sandhill Crane *Grus canadensis*

DESCRIPTION Gray overall; cap red; legs and neck very long.
SIZE Length to 41" (103 cm).
NESTING **Nest:** On a mound rising above water or on dry ground, made from plant material. **Eggs:** Normally 2, olive mottled with gray or brown.
HABITAT Marshes, bogs, swamps and meadows.

The sandhill crane is both a migrant and a summer resident. The migratory flights of this bird are memorable: they circle as they gain great heights, often in good voice. The distinctive musical trumpeting calls are easy to identify and can be heard more than a mile away. This crane is well known for its courtship ballet, a series of graceful jumps, which it frequently conducts while on migration. Young sandhill cranes remain with their parents for up to 10 months.

**Birding Tip:** To differentiate cranes from herons in flight, remember that cranes fly with their necks stretched out while herons hold their necks in an S shape. (See p. 17)

# Semipalmated Plover *Charadrius semipalmatus*

**DESCRIPTION** Back dark brown; breast white with a single black necklace; legs bright yellow-orange.
**SIZE** Length to 7 ½" (19 cm).
**NESTING** **Nest:** On the ground, often on an island. Nest is a shallow depression in sand or gravel. **Eggs:** Normally 4, olive with brown blotches.
**HABITAT** Salt water and fresh water sites.

The semipalmated plover is a locally abundant migrant and summer visitor along much of the outer coast. Most breeding occurs in Alaska and northern Canada. This bird frequents a variety of shorelines, including sandy beaches, mud flats and flooded fields, but it prefers the coast. It often calls with a double whistle while in flight. Some individuals migrate long distances, from as far away as South America. "Semipalmated" refers to the partially webbed toes of the bird.

# Killdeer *Charadrius vociferus*

**DESCRIPTION** Back dark brown; breast white with a double black necklace; rump reddish orange.
**SIZE** Length to 10 ½" (26 cm).
**NESTING** **Nest:** On the ground, in an open area. Nest is a depression, sometimes lined with pebbles, grass or twigs. **Eggs:** Typically 4, buff with black or brown blotches.
**HABITAT** A wide variety of wetlands, open fields, pastures and occasionally the seashore.

*Adult warms its young.*

The killdeer, a plover, is a year-round resident along the coast and one of the earliest spring migrants to interior habitats. It places its eggs in a depression on bare ground, and both parents incubate the eggs and care for their young. The killdeer is renowned for its "broken wing" behavior to distract possible predators from the nest. When other dangers are present, such as grazing mammals that might step on the nest, the killdeer's defense is much different: it stands over the nest and scolds the intruder in order to drive it away.

# Black Oystercatcher *Haematopus bachmani*

**DESCRIPTION Adult:** Black overall; eyes yellow; bill bright red.
**SIZE** Length to 18 ½" (46 cm).
**NESTING Nest:** In a rock depression or on gravel, lined with pebbles and shells. **Eggs:** Normally 2–3, buff with dark scribbles and blotches.
**HABITAT** Rocky coastal areas.

The black oystercatcher is a striking and often vocal year-round resident. It uses its long bill to probe for marine invertebrates such as plate limpets, shield limpets, black Katy chitons, Pacific blue mussels and, yes, oysters. Researchers have determined that it takes the black oystercatcher a mere 10 seconds to remove and devour a limpet, while it takes an average of 130 seconds to open a large Pacific oyster.

Several predators, including the common raven (see p. 68) and northwestern crow (p. 68), are known to steal eggs from the nest of the black oystercatcher. This predation has caused some individuals to re-nest up to 5 times in one season.

---

# Greater Yellowlegs *Tringa melanoleuca*

**DESCRIPTION Adult:** Back and wings gray to brown; legs yellow or orange; bill long, slender and slightly upturned.
**SIZE** Length to 14" (35 cm).
**NESTING Nest:** On the ground, near water, in a swampy wooded area of the north. Nest is made in a depression sparsely lined with grasses. **Eggs:** Normally 4, buff with gray and brown blotches.
**HABITAT** Fresh water and salt water shores.

The greater yellowlegs is commonly observed while on migration to and from its breeding grounds in the north.

**Similar Species:** Birders find it a challenge to distinguish this bird from a smaller and very similar species, the lesser yellowlegs (*Tringa flavipes*). When the two species are side by side, the size differences are clear. The bill of the greater yellowlegs is also longer and upturned; about 1 ⅓ as long as the head, while the bill of the lesser yellowlegs is about the same length as its head. The calls of the two species also differ: the greater yellowlegs' call is *whew-whew-whew*, while that of the lesser is a simple *tu tu*.

# Spotted Sandpiper *Actitis macularia*

**DESCRIPTION** Head and back brown; breast spotted.
**SIZE** Length to 7 ½" (19 cm).
**NESTING Nest:** On the ground. Nest is a depression lined with grass and moss. **Eggs:** Normally 4, buff with brown blotches.
**HABITAT** Primarily near fresh water.

The spotted sandpiper is a common summer resident along the shores of lakes, rivers, streams and various types of marshes. Although this species may be observed in small flocks during migration, individuals are often found alone, walking with a distinctive "teetering" motion.

Researchers have found that in some areas, where there is an abundance of males, the female spotted sandpiper lays a clutch of eggs and then leaves it with the male to incubate and raise the young. She then takes up residence with another male and lays a second clutch of eggs for that male to raise. She may repeat the pattern with as many as 5 males before settling down to remain with her "chosen one."

# Surfbird *Aphriza virgata*

**DESCRIPTION Summer:** Brown spotted with black; scapulars rufous; bill short and yellowish; legs greenish yellow. **Winter:** Gray overall; lower breast white.
**SIZE** Length to 10" (25 cm).
**NESTING Nest:** On dry ground. Nest materials include dead leaves and moss. **Eggs:** Normally 4, buff with reddish brown spots.
**HABITAT** Rocky coastal areas.

"Surf's up" in the world of the surfbird. It is often found at the edge of the water, where the surf laps at its feet. This bird is a common winter visitor along the coast and is also observed on migration to its breeding range in the alpine areas of Alaska and the Yukon. This species can often be observed in small flocks in the intertidal zone, feeding on barnacles, limpets, snails, mussels and a variety of other marine organisms. To feed, it uses its thick bill to detach marine creatures from rocks and other hard surfaces.

# Sanderling *Calidris alba*

DESCRIPTION **Summer:** Upper parts reddish brown; underparts white. **Winter:** Pale overall; back gray; belly white.
SIZE Length to 8" (20 cm).
NESTING **Nest:** On the ground, in an open area. Nest is a slight depression, often lined with leaves. **Eggs:** Normally 4, olive to brown with a few brown and black spots.
HABITAT Primarily sandy beaches.

This common winter resident and migrant nests in the Arctic regions of North America, Europe and Asia. It is a delightful species, probably our palest shorebird, and it can be found on every continent at some time or another during the year. Like many shorebirds, each flock performs an aerial ballet that is not soon forgotten. Sanderlings prefer to feed on hard-packed sand beaches during the ebb or receding tide. They have also been observed feeding at midnight under the light of the moon. Perhaps that is because they are romantics, but it is more likely that a low tide occurred at that time.

# Western Sandpiper *Calidris mauri*

DESCRIPTION Brown overall; wings rufous at base of the scapulars; head with rufous markings; legs and feet black; bill long, pointed and drooping slightly at tip.
SIZE Length to 6 ½" (16 cm).
NESTING **Nest:** On the ground, often under a shrub. Nest is a depression lined with sedges, leaves and lichens. **Eggs:** Normally 4, whitish to brown with dark brown blotches.
HABITAT Salt water and fresh water beaches, especially mud flats.

The western sandpiper is the most abundant shorebird along the Pacific Northwest coast. Flocks are often seen in spring and fall, flying in unison. Large volumes of high-energy food are required for the thousands of sandpipers that migrate from Peru to the Arctic and back again each year. Like most sandpipers, this species rests with one leg tucked up, making it look as though every bird in the entire group is one-legged. If disturbed, all the birds often hop on one leg rather than using two legs to move.

**Similar Species:** The semipalmated sandpiper (*Calidris pusilla*) is a very similar species. It is paler overall, with a short, blunt bill and just a touch of rufous at base of the scapulars in the spring breeding plumage.

# Least Sandpiper *Calidris minutilla*

**DESCRIPTION** Back dark brown; bill short; legs short and yellowish.
**SIZE** Length to 6" (15 cm).
**NESTING** Nest: On the ground, near water. Nest is a depression lined with grass. Eggs: Normally 4, buff with brown blotches.
**HABITAT** Salt water and fresh water beaches.

The least sandpiper is the smallest sandpiper in the world. It is a common species that is found in wetlands throughout the region during migration. The birds typically roost individually or in small groups, and nest from western Alaska to Labrador. At mudflats and sand beaches, they feed on worms, small crustaceans and a variety of insects. The least sandpiper is sometimes called a "peep," a term used for any small sandpiper, especially when its identity is in question.

# Dunlin *Calidris alpina*

**DESCRIPTION Summer:** Back reddish; wings brown; belly with large, black patch; bill heavy with a drooping tip. **Winter:** Grayish brown overall.
**SIZE** Length to 8 ½" (21 cm).
**NESTING Nest:** On the ground. Nest is a slight depression lined with grass and leaves. **Eggs:** Normally 4, olive with brown blotches, especially at larger end.
**HABITAT** Gravel, sand and mud beaches.

The dunlin is one of the most abundant shorebirds found along the Pacific coast in winter. During its migration to its northern breeding grounds in the Arctic, this species travels in flocks numbering into the tens of thousands. It feeds along a variety of shorelines, and can be found inland on lakes, rivers, sloughs and similar wetlands. The dunlin is also one of the shorebirds renowned for its spectacular group aerial ballets, in which it may be accompanied by the sanderling (see p. 46).

# Short-billed Dowitcher *Limnodromus griseus*

**DESCRIPTION Summer:** Upper parts dark brown; underparts reddish; bill long and straight. **Winter:** Upper parts brownish gray; breast gray; underparts white. **SIZE** Length to 11" (28 cm). **NESTING Nest:** On the ground, often near water in the north, lined with grasses and sedges. Bottom of nest is often wet. **Eggs:** Normally 3–4, olive with brown markings. **HABITAT** Fresh water and salt water shores.

Like all shorebirds, the short-billed dowitcher constantly probes the shoreline for its dinner. This preoccupation with feeding sometimes allows viewers to observe the bird at close range. Foods include a variety of marine worms, as well as mollusks and insects. Reports suggest that the female leaves the male to care for the young once they have hatched. The call of this bird is a distinctive *tu tu tu*.

**Similar Species:** The long-billed dowitcher (*Limnodromus scolopaceus*) is very similar but has a distinctive *keek* call. Despite their common names, these birds do not differ reliably in the length of their bills—both species have long bills. The long-billed dowitcher is often observed during the winter months, unlike the migratory short-billed dowitcher.

# Common Snipe *Gallinago gallinago*

**DESCRIPTION** Brown overall; back striped; bill very long and straight. **SIZE** Length to 10 ½" (26 cm). **NESTING Nest:** On the ground. Nesting materials include leaves, grass and moss. **Eggs:** Normally 4, buff with dark brown blotches. **HABITAT** Marshlands and grassy meadows.

Common snipe are year-round residents and world citizens. Both males and females are well known for "whinnying" during their roller-coaster courtship display. This distinctive sound is created when air rushes through their stiff outer tail feathers as they dive. The common snipe is a solitary species that uses its long bill to probe for earthworms, one of its main foods. It also feeds on cutworms, leeches, grasshoppers, beetles, mosquitoes and other insects. The common snipe is normally very stealthy when not displaying, so it can startle you if you happen to flush one.

# Wilson's Phalarope *Phalaropus tricolor*

**DESCRIPTION Summer:** Back and wings dark; chin white; broad dark bar runs through the eye and continues down the side of the neck toward the back; bill long and narrow. **Winter:** Back and wings gray; underparts white; thin gray line through eye.
**SIZE** Length to 9 ¼" (23 cm).
**NESTING Nest:** On the ground, near water. Nest is a simple scrape lined with a few grasses.
**Eggs:** Normally 4, buff with brown blotches.
**HABITAT** Marshes, ponds and mud flats.

In the world of the Wilson's phalarope, females compete for males and a single female may mate with more than one male. In fact, the

*Female in summer plumage.*

female is also more aggressive than the male during courtship activities. Young Wilson's phalaropes, like all phalaropes, are precocial (advanced in their development) and are able to swim at the amazing age of one hour. This species nests in local wetlands, whereas the red-necked phalarope (see below) just migrates through the area. Both species feed by using the "spinning" technique (see below), and both migrate south, spending their winters in South America.

# Red-necked Phalarope *Phalaropus lobatus*

*Female in summer plumage.*

**DESCRIPTION Summer:** Overall dark; chin white; neck dark gray with bright reddish brown patch on side. **Winter:** Back and wings gray; underparts white; black bar through eye.
**SIZE** Length to 7 ¾" (19.5 cm).
**NESTING Nest:** On the ground, near water. Nest is a simple scrape. **Eggs:** Normally 4, olive with dark brown blotches.
**HABITAT** Lakes and large wetlands.

Phalaropes are famous for their "spinning" feeding technique. By swimming in tight circles with their lobed toes, they draw up various invertebrates to the water's surface and quickly dine upon them. Phalaropes are also well known for their reversed gender roles. The females are the more brightly colored, and once the eggs are laid, they leave the more subtly colored male to incubate the eggs and brood the young in the Arctic. Phalaropes are also polyandrous: the female mates with several males and lays eggs for each to incubate. The red-necked phalarope is normally observed during its migration to the Arctic from Peru and vice versa.

# Bonaparte's Gull *Larus philadelphia*

**DESCRIPTION Summer:** White overall; mantle gray; head black; bill black; legs red. **Winter:** Head white with a black spot at the ear.
**SIZE** Length to 14" (35 cm).
**NESTING Nest:** In a coniferous tree, 4–20' (1–6 m) off the ground. **Eggs:** Normally 3, olive with brown blotches.
**HABITAT** Near fresh water and salt water.

*Summer.*

The Bonaparte's gull is commonly seen along the coast during migration in flocks numbering into the hundreds. It is also found inland, but in smaller numbers. The juvenile resembles the winter adult, but has a dark band on the secondary feathers. The bird acquires the black head of its adult plumage in its second year.

The diet of this small gull is determined largely by its habitat. Inland birds are mainly insectivorous, while those along the coast feed on small fish, shrimp, marine worms and crustaceans. These dainty gulls are always a delight to watch as they feed at the edge of the water during migration.

*Winter.*

# Mew Gull *Larus canus*

DESCRIPTION **Adult:** Back and wings blue-gray; head white and rounded; bill narrow and yellow; eyes dark.
SIZE Length to 16" (40 cm).
NESTING **Nest:** On the ground near shoreline, or in a tree to 20' (6 m) off the ground. **Eggs:** Normally 3, olive with brown blotches.
HABITAT Near fresh water and salt water.

The mew gull is a dainty species that feeds on fish, worms, insects and a variety of other gourmet items. It is noticeably smaller than most gull species observed in the Pacific Northwest, and it is light and buoyant in flight. Although this species is a common migrant and winter visitor, it is not commonly seen during the summer.

This gull makes two calls, one that is sometimes described as *kyah kyah*, and another, *meew meew*, which inspired its common name.

# Ring-billed Gull *Larus delawarensis*

DESCRIPTION **Breeding adult:** White overall with gray mantle; wing tips black; eyes and legs yellow; bill yellow with a black ring near the tip. **Juvenile:** Head and breast streaked with gray.
SIZE Length to 17 ½" (44 cm).
NESTING **Nest:** On the ground, often on an island, in colonies. Nest is made from grass, weeds and moss. **Eggs:** Normally 2–4, light brown with dark brown blotches.
HABITAT Fresh water and salt water areas, parks and fields.

The ring-billed gull is common in both coastal and interior regions. Some individuals live here all year round, but most migrate to warmer climes during the winter months. Like many gulls, this one prefers to nest on islands, frequently nesting with other species such as the California gull (p. 52) and herring gull (p. 52). This species was not always as common as it is today; it is a scavenger and the growing amount of human refuse has greatly aided in expanding its numbers. In fact, it is the most abundant gull found in North America.

# California Gull *Larus californicus*

**DESCRIPTION Breeding adult:** Back and wings blue-gray; wing tips black; bill yellow with red spot on lower bill; legs greenish to yellowish. This combination distinguishes the California gull from other species. **First year immature:** Head and body dark brown; bill pink with black tip; legs pink.
**SIZE** Length to 21" (53 cm).
**NESTING Nest:** On the ground, often on an island, in colonies. Nest is made from grass and weeds, and lined with feathers. **Eggs:** Normally 2–3, buff, olive or brown with dark brown blotches.
**HABITAT** Along the coast, near lakes, on farmlands and in urban centers.

The California gull is an omnivore, feeding on a wide range of items including insects, fish, refuse, and the eggs and young of other birds. This species came to the rescue of Mormon settlers in Salt Lake City in 1848, when a plague of grasshoppers threatened their crops. Today it is sometimes seen following the farmer's plow, feeding on insects. The California gull winters along the California and Baja California coast.

# Herring Gull *Larus argentatus*

*Juvenile.*

**DESCRIPTION Breeding adult:** Body large and white; mantle gray; wing tips black; feet pink; eye yellow; bill yellow with red spot at tip. **Juvenile:** Overall mottled brown; legs and feet pink; bill dark or yellow with black tip.
**SIZE** Length to 25" (63 cm).
**NESTING Nest:** On the ground, in colonies. Nest is made from grasses and seaweed. **Eggs:** Normally 3, buff with brown blotches.
**HABITAT** Salt water and fresh water areas.

Often described as "mean-looking," this gull is a year-round resident along the coast, and is commonly found throughout much of the Pacific Northwest during the warmer months of the year. A full 4 years are required for the bird to acquire its adult plumage. The herring gull ranges from sea level to 5,528' (1,660 m) and always nests in colonies near water. It is known to mate occasionally with other gulls, including the glaucous-winged gull (see p. 53). In the 19th century, this gull was hunted for its eggs and feathers.

**Similar Species:** The thayer's gull (*Larus thayeri*) is a similar-looking species often seen along the coast. Its eyes are dark rather than yellow.

# Glaucous-winged Gull *Larus glaucescens*

**DESCRIPTION Adult:** White overall; mantle gray; wing tips white; feet and legs pink; bill yellow with red spot on lower bill. **Juvenile:** Overall gray-brown, bill black.
**SIZE** Length to 27" (68 cm).
**NESTING Nest:** On the ground or on a cliff or roof, in colonies. **Eggs:** Normally 2–3, olive with brown scribbles and blotches.
**HABITAT** Salt water and fresh water areas.

The glaucous-winged gull is the most common gull observed along the coast of the Pacific Northwest. The diet of this species varies greatly, from fries at the local fast food outlet to more natural items such as sea stars, which are foraged from the seashore. This gull, an opportunist, also dines on such things as birds' eggs, Pacific blue mussels, sea urchins, barnacles and fish, to name just a few. Glaucous-winged gulls sometimes feed on clams contaminated with PSP or red tide; remarkably, they regurgitate these clams soon after swallowing them. Banding studies have shown this species to live to at least 22 years.

**Similar Species:** The western gull (*Larus occidentalis*) is a similar-looking species with a larger bill and a dark gray back and wings. The glaucous-winged gull often hybridizes with the western gull.

# Caspian Tern *Sterna caspia*

**DESCRIPTION Summer:** White overall; cap solid black; bill heavy and red; legs black. **Winter:** Cap black, mixed with some white.
**SIZE** Length to 21" (53 cm).
**NESTING Nest:** On the ground, solitary or in colonies. Nest is a scrape with a lining of grasses and seaweed. **Eggs:** Normally 1–3, pale buff with brown or black spots.
**HABITAT** Protected bays along the coast and fresh water bodies with small fish.

The Caspian tern is a large summer visitor that has dramatically expanded its range in recent years. On the West Coast, nesting colonies were once found only at sheltered sites in California. Now, large colonies have been established in protected bays along the coast of Washington, and it is expected to become more common in the Pacific Northwest. This bird is North America's largest tern. It has an impressive wingspan of 50" (1.2 m) and a distinctive loud, raspy, grating *kraaa* call. Individuals live as long as 12 years, occasionally 17 years.

# Common Tern *Sterna hirundo*

**DESCRIPTION** White overall; cap black; tail long; wings with a black wedge mark on upper surface; bill and legs red.
**SIZE** Length to 14 ½" (36 cm).
**NESTING Nest:** In a scrape on the ground, lined with plant material. **Eggs:** Normally 1–3, buff or pale blue with brown speckles.
**HABITAT** Salt water and fresh water areas.

Like all terns, the common tern differs from gulls—its close relatives—in that it dives head first into the water to catch small fish. This is a small tern that feeds primarily on fish, but it also takes advantage of other food items such as shrimp and even the occasional swallowtail butterfly. Common terns are often seen while on migration to and from their breeding grounds in Alberta, east to Newfoundland. They are delicate-looking birds, very buoyant, with a butterfly-like flight pattern.

**Similar Species:** The Arctic tern (*Sterna paradisaea*) is very similar in appearance, but it has a longer tail and lacks the black wedge mark on the upper wing. This tern may be seen while on migration to or from its nesting areas, in the Arctic and in one area in Washington.

# Pigeon Guillemot *Cepphus columba*

**DESCRIPTION Breeding:** Overall black; wings with white triangular patch; bill long and black. **Winter:** Overall white; back and wings mottled black.
**SIZE** Length to 13 ½" (34 cm).
**NESTING Nest:** Among boulders or in a burrow. Nest is a mere scrape in the dirt. Nest sites are often reused for several years. **Eggs:** Normally 1–2, cream colored to greenish with gray or brown blotches.
**HABITAT** Rocky shores and inshore waters.

The pigeon guillemot, which resembles a seabird dressed in a formal tux, is an agile species that dives to 150' (45 m) below the surface to forage for its food on the sea bottom. It uses its wings primarily to propel itself underwater and uses its feet for both steering and propulsion. Preferred foods include small fish, shrimps, crabs, marine worms and mollusks, as well as small octopus.

# Rock Dove *Columba livia*

**DESCRIPTION** Highly variable; normally back and wings gray; head dark gray; neck iridescent.
**SIZE** Length to 12 ½" (31 cm).
**NESTING Nest:** On a man-made structure. Nest materials include twigs and grass. **Eggs:** Normally 2, white.
**HABITAT** Urban environments.

The rock dove, also called pigeon, was introduced by European settlers over a century ago and is now found over much of North America. Members of the pigeon and dove family are unique in that both male and female adult birds can produce a "milk" in their digestive systems and feed it to their young.

This bird played an important role in saving the Peregrine falcon (see p. 37) from extinction. Because the rock dove lives in cities, it was not contaminated with DDT and similar pesticides, as was other prey of the Peregrine falcon. Those Peregrines that nested in high-rise buildings in large cities were able to safely feed on rock doves.

# Mourning Dove *Zenaida macroura*

**DESCRIPTION** Body slender; overall brown; under parts pinkish; tail long and pointed.
**SIZE** Length to 12" (30 cm).
**NESTING Nest:** On the ground or in a tree, normally to 40' (12 m) off the ground. Nest is flimsy and made from sticks. **Eggs:** Normally 2, white.
**HABITAT** Semi-open areas.

The distinctive song of the mourning dove, a sad-sounding cooing: *oowoo-woo-woo-woo*, is likely the origin of its common name. This dove feeds on the seeds of grasses and wildflowers. Like all birds that eat seeds, this one regularly swallows grit or small gravel to aid in digestion. In the northern limit of its range, to central B.C., the mourning dove raises a single brood per year. In the south, however (across the southern U.S.), an amazing 6 broods may be produced within one year.

# Barn Owl *Tyto alba*

**DESCRIPTION Male:** Light-colored overall; face heart-shaped; eyes dark. **Female:** Darker overall.
**SIZE** Length to 16" (40 cm).
**NESTING Nest:** In a barn, cave, hollow tree or similar location. No nest is actually made. **Eggs:** Normally 3–8, whitish.
**HABITAT** Chiefly agricultural areas.

Barn owls nest in buildings such as barns, and are also known to nest in large tree cavities and to accept nest boxes constructed especially for them. This species is restricted to areas with mild winters. Its numbers have declined steadily as agricultural land has been given over to development. The bird is an important predator in such areas, feeding on mice and voles. It is most frequently observed at dusk, and its voice has been described as a raspy, hissing screech.

# Great Horned Owl *Bubo virginianus*

**DESCRIPTION** Back and wings dark brown; throat white; ear tufts widely spaced; eyes yellow.
**SIZE** Length to 22" (55 cm).
**NESTING Nest:** In the abandoned nest of a hawk, eagle or crow, 20–60' (6–18 m) off the ground, usually with no new nest materials added. **Eggs:** Normally 2–3, whitish.
**HABITAT** Forested areas.

The great horned owl gets its name from the two tufts of feathers on its head. It is a large species and one of the earliest of all nesters, with incubation beginning in late February or early March. A person who ventures too close to an active nest may be attacked by an angry adult, which may draw blood. This owl feeds on a wide variety of mammals, including porcupines and skunks. It is a fearsome, determined hunter that is undeterred by quills and foul smells. Great horned owls hunt by dusk and by night, and smaller owl species also become the hunted.

# Northern Pygmy-owl *Glaucidium gnoma*

**DESCRIPTION** Brown above; crown spotted; underparts streaked; eyes yellow; tail long.
**SIZE** Length to 6 ¾" (17 cm).
**NESTING Nest:** In a hollow tree, often in an opening made by a woodpecker, 8–25' (2.5–8 m) off the ground. **Eggs:** Normally 3–4, white.
**HABITAT** Forested areas.

The northern pygmy-owl is often observed sitting on top of a tree while being mobbed by small birds, which gather and fly at the owl in order to chase it away. In fact, that is often the manner in which birders locate this owl. Eventually the mobbing stops and the owl goes back to sleep. This bird is a predator, active at dusk and dawn and feeding principally on small birds. Two eye-like spots or nape spots are found on the back of the head.

**Patience has its rewards!** This northern pygmy-owl was observed for some time before being mobbed by a group of small birds. This remarkable photograph shows its response to this mobbing behaviour in an attempt to make itself appear fierce.

57

# Barred Owl Strix varia

**DESCRIPTION** Brown above; facial disk prominent; eyes dark; belly with vertical streaks.
**SIZE** Length to 21" (53 cm).
**NESTING Nest:** In a natural tree hollow, the abandoned nest of a hawk or crow, or a similar location. **Eggs:** Normally 2–3, white.
**HABITAT** Forested areas.

This common year-round resident occurs in forested areas throughout much of eastern North America and is rapidly expanding its range. Its voice is a distinctive sequence of hoots: *who-cooks-for-you, who-cooks-for-you-all.* Juveniles, however, emit a loud and distinctive *psssssst*, which can be heard between June and August. This call aids birders greatly in locating the barred owl. Diet is primarily forest birds and mice, but this owl also eats reptiles, fish and insects. It is one of the easier forest owls to locate because it often hunts during the day.

**Similar Species:** Another dark-eyed species, the spotted owl (*Strix occidentalis*), lives only in old-growth forests. It is a rare species that can be identified by the white spots on the chest and crown.

# Long-eared Owl Asio otus

**DESCRIPTION** Back and wings dark brown; facial disk rufous; ear tufts closely spaced.
**SIZE** Length to 15" (38 cm).
**NESTING Nest:** In the abandoned nest of a hawk, eagle or crow, 4–30' (1–9 m) off the ground, with no nest materials added. **Eggs:** Normally 4–6, white.
**HABITAT** Trees near open areas.

This slender owl often goes unnoticed during the day as it sits quietly in a thicket or dense stand of trees. It feeds during the night, primarily on small mammals such as voles. Like all owls, it regurgitates pellets containing the indigestible bones and fur of its prey, which makes it easy to determine the bird's diet. This owl incubates its eggs as soon as they are laid, so the young vary greatly in age. In fact, one family might consist of some down-covered young in the nest, and others that are learning to fly. The long-eared owl can be found between central B.C. and northern Baja California, Mexico.

# Short-eared Owl *Asio flammeus*

**DESCRIPTION** Back and wings brown; face round; tufts present but small and rarely seen; underside heavily streaked, belly buff.
**SIZE** Length to 15" (38 cm).
**NESTING Nest:** On dry ground, often near a marsh. Nest materials include grass and feathers. **Eggs:** Normally 3–11, white.
**HABITAT** Open meadows and wetlands.

The short-eared owl is a year-round resident that nests in open areas. Its flight is irregular and moth-like. The male executes an impressive courtship ritual using his wings to perform a clapping display. During the winter months, as owls seek out suitable hunting areas, accumulations of several owls may occur. Individuals sit on vantage points, patiently waiting for the slightest movement in order to capture their next meal, often by daylight. The owls remain in an area only as long as the food supply holds.

# Northern Saw-whet Owl *Aegolius acadicus*

**DESCRIPTION Adult:** Brown above; streaked underparts; crown with short stripes; eyes yellow, tail short. **Juvenile:** Overall reddish; large white area between the eyes.
**SIZE** Length to 8" (20 cm).
**NESTING Nest:** In a hollow tree, often in an opening made by a woodpecker, 15–60' (4.5–18 m) off the ground. **Eggs:** Normally 5–6, white.
**HABITAT** Forested areas.

The northern saw-whet owl is a common owl that easily goes undetected. Its small size and its habit of sleeping during the day in a shrub or tree aid it greatly in being unnoticed. The observer who does happen to see one will find that this owl is one of the few birds that allows a person to get near it.

During winter, the northern saw-whet owl has been known to capture more food than it can eat at one time, then store it in a nearby tree, where it freezes. Later, the owl thaws the food using the warmth of its body.

# Common Nighthawk *Chordeiles minor*

**DESCRIPTION Male:** Body and wings dark gray with barring; wings pointed with white patch (pronounced in flight); tail with white bar. **Female:** Throat yellow; tail lacking white bar.
**SIZE** Length to 9 ½" (24 cm).
**NESTING Nest:** On the ground or on a flat-topped building. No actual nest is built. **Eggs:** Normally 2, buff with brown blotches.
**HABITAT** A wide variety of open areas and rooftops.

The nighthawk is often heard long before it is observed. Its distinctive call has been described as a nasal *peent*. The bird's long, slender wings give it the agility necessary to capture insects in flight, and it has a relatively large mouth to help catch insects on the wing. The nighthawk is a summer resident, and in October it makes its way south to winter hideaways in Mexico and Central America. The numbers of this species are declining in parts of its range, perhaps because of pesticide use or habitat loss.

# Calliope Hummingbird *Stellula calliope*

**DESCRIPTION Adult:** Upper parts greenish. **Male:** Throat streaked with purple-red. **Female:** Flanks light cinnamon; throat speckled with green.
**SIZE** Length to 3 ¼" (8 cm).
**NESTING Nest:** In a conifer, 6–40' (2–12 m) off the ground. Nest is made of plant down, moss, lichens and/or other materials, bound together with spider webs. **Eggs:** Normally 2, white.
**HABITAT** Open mountain woodlands, wooded pond edges, canyons and similar situations.

The courtship antics of the male Calliope hummingbird include impressive pendulum-style swoops toward the female. The male remains with the female only until nesting begins, then moves on to other areas. This hummingbird is primarily a summer resident of the mountains, but it has also been found nesting in gardens and orchards. It defends its territory fiercely, uttering a series of squeaks.

# Rufous Hummingbird *Selasphorus rufus*

**DESCRIPTION Male:** Back reddish brown; tail rufous; throat iridescent reddish orange.
**Female:** Tail rufous.
**SIZE** Length to 3 ¾" (9 cm).
**NESTING Nest:** In a conifer, 3–30' (1–9 m) off the ground. Nest is made of plant down, moss, lichens and/or other materials, bound together with spider webs. **Eggs:** Normally 2, white.
**HABITAT** Forest edges, mountain meadows and shores of streams.

*Female and young.*

Arriving with the first blossoms of spring, the rufous hummingbird is a true bundle of energy. The male can be observed performing dive bombs in order to impress a chosen female hidden on a lower branch. This bird's tiny nest holds 2 tiny pea-sized eggs. The young grow quickly and eventually become big enough to fill the nest completely, reshaping it as they reach fledgling size. Like all hummingbirds, this species can fly forward, fly backward and hover. As they fly from one blossom to another, these tiny jewels feed on nectar and small insects. They are strongly attracted to hummingbird feeders that simulate red flowers in the wild. The rufous is also an aggressive species that has little tolerance for other hummingbirds. This is why people often place several nectar feeders in one area to let all hummingbirds feed.

*Male.*

# Belted Kingfisher *Ceryle alcyon*

**DESCRIPTION Male:** Overall blue-gray above and whitish below with a blue-gray necklace. **Female:** Lower breast displays an orange band.
**SIZE** Length to 14" (35 cm).
**NESTING Nest:** A burrow in a bank near water, excavated by the belted kingfisher. No nest materials are added. **Eggs:** Normally 6–7, white.
**HABITAT** Fresh water and salt water areas.

The kingfisher is distinctive for its loud, raucous, rattle-like call. It is an expert fisher, adept at catching a meal by diving into the water and emerging with a small fish. The bird then returns to its favorite perch to beat the fish on a branch, and often to toss it in the air and catch it head first. Like owls, kingfishers cough up pellets containing the indigestible portions of their meals. In addition to fish, they feed on squid, crabs, clams, insects and mice.

# Red-breasted Sapsucker *Sphyrapicus ruber*

**DESCRIPTION** Head, nape and breast bright red; back black with spots; wings black with white patch; belly yellow-striped at edges.
**SIZE** Length to 8 ½" (21 cm).
**NESTING Nest:** In a tree cavity, 50–60' (15–18 m) off the ground. **Eggs:** Normally 3–6, white.
**HABITAT** Forest areas.

The sapsucker clan got its name from the birds' dining etiquette of drilling holes in trees, then returning to collect the beads of sap produced at the chisel holes and the insects that have stuck to it. They do not actually suck sap, but they do feed on sap with their specialized tongues. These year-round residents excavate their own nest holes in trees, which provide nesting sites for many other tree-hole-nesting species.

*The distinctive drilling pattern left by this species.*

62

# Downy Woodpecker *Picoides pubescens*

**DESCRIPTION** Wings black with white spots; head black with white stripes; breast and belly white; bill slender and less than half the length of the head; outer tail feathers white with a few black bars. **Male:** Nape with red bar. **Female:** Nape without red bar.
**SIZE** Length to 6" (15 cm).
**NESTING Nest:** Usually in a cavity of a dead tree, 12–30' (3.5–9 m) off the ground. **Eggs:** Normally 4–5, white.
**HABITAT** Forested areas.

This year-round resident is North America's smallest woodpecker. Its bill is narrower and shorter than that of the similar-looking hairy woodpecker (below). Both male and female help to excavate a nesting cavity, as well as incubate the eggs and feed their young. During the fall and winter, males and females feed in separate territories, and both select dead limbs on which to drum loudly, thus advertising their presence. Diet includes a wide range of insects, especially beetles and ants, and these birds frequent suet feeders during the winter months.

# Hairy Woodpecker *Picoides villosus*

**DESCRIPTION** Wings black with white spots; head black with white stripes; breast and belly white; bill thickened and long-almost ¾ the length of the head; outer tail feathers white only. **Male:** Nape with red patch. **Female:** Nape without red patch.
**SIZE** Length to 9 ¼" (23 cm).
**NESTING Nest:** In a tree cavity, 4–60' (1–18 m) off the ground. **Eggs:** Normally 4, white.
**HABITAT** Woodlands.

This year-round resident is common throughout much of North America. Dinner consists mainly of the larvae of various beetles and other insects that live in the wood of trees. Surprisingly, hairy woodpeckers occasionally also feed on fruit and seeds. The birds keep their mates all year, although separate territories are maintained by the sexes. The female normally initiates courtship activities by drumming on one of several favorite drum trees, a sound that is often heard in the fall and can be very intense at times. Human beings can hear the drumming 2,400' (720 m) away. The hairy woodpecker's most common vocalization is *jeek, jeek*, often used as a greeting, or it can be described as a hard *peek* (perhaps easier to remember). Courtship flights may be observed: a pair flies duet style, with one bird taking the lead, then the other.

# Northern Flicker *Colaptes auratus*

**DESCRIPTION** Back and wings brown barred with black; belly buff, spotted with black; rump white, very noticeable when bird is in flight; bib black. **Male:** Moustache red.
**SIZE** Length to 12 ½" (31 cm).
**NESTING Nest:** In a cavity of a dead tree, 6–20' (1.8–6 m) off the ground.
**Eggs:** Normally 5–8, white.
**HABITAT** Moderately open areas.

The northern flicker often forages for snacks on the ground or in ants' nests. In fact, in the bird world it is the champion for eating ants. Scientists determined in at least one study that 45% of all foods consumed by this woodpecker were ants. One individual was found to have more than 5,000 ants in its stomach. Additional food items in the diet included a wide variety of insects and a large selection of fruits. The northern flicker is important in providing nest sites for the bufflehead (see p. 30) and other hole-nesters, which occupy the accommodations once the flickers have finished with them.

# Pileated Woodpecker *Dryocopus pileatus*

**DESCRIPTION** Back and wings black; head black with white stripes and red crest. **Male:** Moustache red.
**SIZE** Length to 16 ½" (41 cm).
**NESTING Nest:** In a cavity of a live or dead tree, 15–80' (4.5–24 m) off the ground. No nest materials are added.
**Eggs:** Normally 3–5, white.
**HABITAT** Mature forests. This species requires large trees for nesting.

"Prehistoric" may best describe the appearance of this large, primitive-looking bird. Its loud, powerful voice makes a sound that could be described as *wucka-wucka-wucka*. The pileated woodpecker is also known for its bursts of drumming, which can be heard at long distances. When foraging, this bird leaves a distinctive calling card. It chisels out large, distinctive rectangular holes while it feeds, primarily on ants living in the trunks of trees. Pairs of pileated woodpeckers remain together year-round and often return to the same area to nest for years. The nest is normally, but not always, chosen so that it faces either east or south. This bird is often easily approached.

*The distinctive excavation left by this species.*

# Willow Flycatcher *Empidonax traillii*

**DESCRIPTION** Upper parts olive-brown; double wing bars; no conspicuous eye-ring; throat white; belly yellowish.
**SIZE** Length to 5 ½" (14 cm).
**NESTING Nest:** In a deciduous tree or shrub, 4–15' (1–4.5 m) off the ground. Nest is made from grass and bark, and lined with plant down.
**Eggs:** Normally 3–4, whitish with brown speckles.
**HABITAT** Thickets and similar areas near water; open riparian and disturbed areas.

The willow flycatcher arrives in May from its wintering area in Central and South America, and often goes undetected until the male proclaims his territory with a distinctive *fitz-bew* "song," the best way to identify this flycatcher.

**Similar Species:** The surest way to distinguish many flycatchers is by voice and habitat. The Pacific slope flycatcher (*Empidonax difficilis*) sings *suwheet* and inhabits coniferous forests. The cordilleran flycatcher (*Empidonax occidentalis*) sings *whee-seet* and occurs in the central interior of the Pacific Northwest. The olive-sided flycatcher (*Contopus cooperi*), well known for its song *quick-three-beers*, prefers high, open slopes. The song of the Hammond's flycatcher (*Empidonax hammondii*) is a rather curt *cha-beck*, and its habitat is primarily open forest gaps and edges.

# Tree Swallow *Tachycineta bicolor*

**DESCRIPTION Adult:** Upper parts dark blue to green; rump dark; underparts white.
**SIZE** Length to 5 ¾" (14.5 cm).
**NESTING Nest:** In a tree cavity, abandoned woodpecker nest or nest box. Nest materials include grass, moss and pine needles; nest is lined with feathers. **Eggs:** Normally 4–7, pale pink to whitish.
**HABITAT** Woodlands near water.

The tree swallow is a tree-hole nester that also adapts to various man-made structures. The installation of nest boxes in many areas, to increase the population of tree swallows, has been very successful. These pleasant birds feed on an amazing number of insects, including beetles, flies, grasshoppers and dragonflies. Surprisingly, they also feed on berries and seeds when insects are less abundant. The bird lives 2.7 years on average, and the longest living individual on record died at age 8.

**Similar Species:** The violet-green swallow (*Tachycineta thalassina*) is a similar swallow, but it has white flank patches that extend to the edge of the rump. Its voice is more chirp-like than the fluid calls of the tree swallow.

# Barn Swallow *Hirundo rustica*

**DESCRIPTION** Back and wings dark blue; throat reddish brown; underparts buff; tail deeply forked.
**SIZE** Length to 6 ¾" (17 cm).
**NESTING Nest:** Usually in a sheltered location, in a man-made structure. Nest is made from mud and grass, and lined with feathers.
**Eggs:** Normally 4–5, white with brown speckles.
**HABITAT** In old buildings and similar structures.

The barn swallow is a common summer resident throughout most of the Pacific Northwest, lingering on the breeding grounds longer than other swallows. One may wonder where the barn swallow nested before human beings provided buildings. Archival field notes and other nesting records show that nesting sites included rock caves, rock cliffs and other natural cavities. These sites may once again become important, as the numbers of barn swallows have declined. Long gone are the days when barns were commonplace—farm and other rural buildings are fewer and farther between.

**Similar Species:** While building its nest, the barn swallow is an excellent mud mason, but the master mud mason of the bird world is the cliff swallow (*Hirundo pyrrhonota*). This remarkable bird uses mud to make a nest in the shape of a bottle (including the neck), which it attaches to a cliff. The cliff swallow has a white belly and rusty cheek patches. Other species similar to the barn swallow include the northern rough-winged swallow (*Stelgidopteryx serripennis*) and bank swallow (*Riparia riparia*), both of which have brown backs and wings.

# Gray Jay *Perisoreus canadensis*

**DESCRIPTION Adult:** Wings, tail and back dark gray; head white with a black patch at the back; breast white. **Juvenile:** Body dark gray.
**SIZE** Length to 11 ½" (29 cm).
**NESTING Nest:** In a conifer, 6–28' (2–8.5 m) off the ground. Nest is made from twigs and bark, and lined with feathers and fur. **Eggs:** Normally 3–4, greenish with brown blotches.
**HABITAT** Generally forests at higher elevations.

This friendly member of the jay clan is familiar to all who travel in the backcountry. It was formerly called the Canada jay, as well as the colloquial names whiskey jack, moose bird and camp robber. The gray jay is widespread and a year-round resident. It nests early in subalpine regions, and incubates its eggs while there is still heavy snow. The young are often fledged about the same time as the snow melts. The gray jay uses its saliva to wrap insects and stick them to branches during the fall and summer, to eat when other food is not abundant.

# Steller's Jay *Cyanocitta stelleri*

**DESCRIPTION** Blue overall; crest black.
**SIZE** Length to 11 ½" (29 cm).
**NESTING Nest:** In a tree or shrub, 10–30'
(3–9 m) off the ground. Nest materials
include twigs, leaves, moss and mud; nest
is lined with fine plant materials. **Eggs:**
Normally 4, greenish speckled with
brown.
**HABITAT** A variety of habitats at lower
elevations.

The Steller's jay is a year-round resident
with a harsh, distinctive call described as
*shaack-shaack-shaack*. This species, the
provincial bird of British Columbia, is
commonly seen at feeders, bringing a
touch of color and much noise. Sometimes it nests near the feeder, a constant food source —
occasionally even just outside a window and well within view!

**Similar Species:** The Steller's jay is often mistaken for the blue jay (*Cyanocitta cristata*), a
similar bird that is blue overall with white patches and a blue crest. The blue jay is a rare
species in this area.

# Clark's Nutcracker *Nucifraga columbiana*

**DESCRIPTION** Body gray; wings black
with white patch; tail black with white
outer feathers.
**SIZE** Length to 12" (30 cm).
**NESTING Nest:** In a coniferous tree, 8-
40' (2.5–12 m) off the ground. Nest is
made from twigs and bark, and lined
with grass and pine needles. **Eggs:**
Normally 2–4, greenish speckled with
brown and gray.
**HABITAT** Mountainous areas above
3,000' (900 m).

Clark's nutcrackers reside in the mountains near timber line. They are omni-
vores, consuming large numbers of seeds,
especially from whitebark and limber
pines, and a wide variety of insects, spiders, small mammals and probably carrion. In one year, an individual normally
hides some 30,000 seeds in 7,500 different spots to eat later, and has a remarkable 70% suc-
cess rate in relocating these seeds. Clark's nutcrackers are opportunists, often on the lookout
for handouts from visitors. But keep in mind that they should only eat natural foods, because
many processed human foods will not give them the nutrients they require.

# American Crow *Corvus brachyrhynchos*

**DESCRIPTION** Black overall; bill slender and smaller than that of the raven; tail rounded.
**SIZE** Length to 17 ½" (44 cm).
**NESTING Nest:** In a tree, 10–70' (3–21 m) off the ground. Nest materials include sticks, mud, weeds, grass and feathers. **Eggs:** Normally 4–6, greenish with brown and gray blotches.
**HABITAT** Areas with mature trees for roosts and nesting.

The American crow is a common migrant and summer resident throughout much of the area. Crows' nests in trees are an important source of nesting sites for a variety of other species, including the great horned owl (see p. 56), merlin (p. 37) and Canada goose (p. 20). The American crow is a smart bird that has with-stood persecution by human beings and continues to thrive.

**Similar Species:** Another smaller species found along the coast, the northwestern crow (*Corvus caurinus*), is considered by some experts to be a subspecies of the American crow.

# Common Raven *Corvus corax*

**DESCRIPTION** Black overall; bill very thick; throat feathers long and pointed; tail wedge-shaped.
**SIZE** Length to 26 ½" (66 cm).
**NESTING Nest:** On a cliff ledge or in a tall tree. Nest is made from sticks and lined with grass, moss and hair. **Eggs:** Normally 4–6, greenish with brown blotches.
**HABITAT** All habitats.

The common raven is a widespread, year-round resident of the Pacific Northwest. Its voice is a hoarse and raspy *kwawk*, compared to that of the American crow, which is more of a *caw*. The raven can also be called the ballet star of the Corvid family (the crow and jay clan). Gliding, soaring, barrel-rolling and diving are all part of ravens' routine, and they seem to enjoy flying. Their courtship rituals, which take place as early as February, also involve aerial antics.

The well-known behaviorist Konrad Lorenz credited the raven as having the "highest mental development" of any species in the bird world. For example, the bird is capable of working alone or in groups to steal food from predator species. One raven may act as a decoy while another grabs the prize. Wild ravens are believed to live as long as 40 years, occasionally even longer.

# Black-capped Chickadee *Poecile atricapilla*

**DESCRIPTION** Cap and bib black; cheeks white.
**SIZE** Length to 5 ¼" (13 cm).
**NESTING Nest:** In a tree cavity or old wood-pecker nest, 5–20' (1.5–6 m) off the ground, or the bird may excavate its own nest cavity.
**Eggs:** Normally 6–8, white with reddish brown speckles.
**HABITAT** Deciduous forests.

This year-round resident is familiar to young and old, and often visits bird feeders. During fall and winter, the black-capped chickadee eats seeds and hides many more. Researchers have determined that the bird grows new brain cells—one cell to remember where it hid each seed. The hippocampus of the brain is used for memory, and new cells replace old ones as they are needed. The black-capped chickadee is known to live as long as 12 years. It is also remarkable for its ability to reduce its body temperature at night by 50–54°F (10–12°C) to save energy.

# Bushtit *Psaltriparus minimus*

**DESCRIPTION** Body gray.
**Male:** Crown brown (coastal birds) or ear patch brown (interior birds).
**SIZE** Length to 4 ½" (11 cm).
**NESTING Nest:** In a tree or shrub, 8–35' (2.5–11 m) off the ground, made of tightly woven grass, moss, leaves, rootlets and twigs, lined with hair and feathers. **Eggs:** Normally 5–7, white.
**HABITAT** Open treed areas and shrubby sites.

The bushtit is well known for its distinctive hanging nest, which resembles a wool sock. This architectural marvel can be as long as 10" (25 cm) and take up to 6 weeks for a pair of birds to build. Some individuals reuse their nests.

This bird consumes a great variety of insects as well as fruit and seeds, and is sometimes observed at feeders. The bushtit can be found from southern B.C. to central Guatemala.

# Red-breasted Nuthatch *Sitta canadensis*

**DESCRIPTION** Cap black; eye-line black; underparts rufous.
**SIZE** Length to 4 ½" (11 cm).
**NESTING Nest:** Excavated in a tree cavity or in an abandoned woodpecker nest, 5–40' (1.5–12 m) off the ground. Nest materials include grass, moss, bark and feathers. **Eggs:** Normally 5–6, white.
**HABITAT** Mature coniferous and mixed-wood forests.

The red-breasted nuthatch, a year-round resident, frequents feeders containing sunflower seeds and suet, but it normally finds its food while moving head first down a tree trunk. This is an industrious species, which digs out its own cavities or occupies a disused woodpecker nest. The bird may smear the entrance to its nest cavity with sap to discourage insects such as ants from entering the nesting chamber. Included in the repertoire of songs is the nasal territorial song *yna-yna-yna*.

# Brown Creeper *Certhia americana*

**DESCRIPTION** Upper parts streaked with brown; underparts white.
**SIZE** Length to 5 ¼" (13 cm).
**NESTING Nest:** Behind tree bark or in a tree cavity, 5–15' (1.5–4.5 m) off the ground. Nest materials include twigs, bark, moss and leaves; nest is lined with feathers. **Eggs:** Normally 5–6, white speckled with reddish brown.
**HABITAT** Mature forests.

The brown creeper searches for insects and spiders by starting low on a tree trunk and working its way up and onto the branches in a spiral pattern. During courtship, the male often chases the female, feeding her as she flutters her wings. The female does all the incubating and brooding of the young, but males help feed the young once they have hatched. Both adults and young hide from predators by pressing their well-camouflaged bodies against the bark of trees. Their song begins with two distinctive notes: *sing! sing!*

# House Wren *Troglodytes aedon*

**DESCRIPTION Adult:** Back and wings dark brown; belly buff; eyebrow faint; tail long.
**SIZE** Length to 4 ¾" (12 cm).
**NESTING Nest:** In any natural or man-made cavity. Nest materials include twigs, grass, animal fur and feathers.
**Eggs:** Normally 6–7, white with reddish brown blotches.
**HABITAT** Open woods, thickets and gardens.

Aptly named, the house wren has a tendency to nest near people's homes, in any available enclosed space such as old woodpecker holes, nest boxes and drainpipes. The male often makes additional dummy nests for the female to choose from. The house sparrow (see p. 87), an introduced species, competes with this native species for nest sites and is believed to be the reason for the decline of the house wren in some areas. The house wren, in turn, is notorious for destroying or removing other birds' eggs. Scientists are uncertain about the reason for this—perhaps they are reducing the competition for food.

# Winter Wren *Troglodytes troglodytes*

**DESCRIPTION** Upper parts reddish brown; lower parts buff-brown with prominent barring; tail very short and often held upright.
**SIZE** Length to 4" (10 cm).
**NESTING Nest:** Any natural cavity up to 6' (1.5 m) off the ground. Nest is made from grass, moss and rootlets, and lined with hair and feathers. **Eggs:** Normally 5–6, white with reddish brown speckles at the large end.
**HABITAT** Forested areas, especially coniferous forests near water.

The winter wren is a wonderfully vociferous addition to our coniferous forests. It is truly a marvelous experience to follow this bird's loud, melodious song and find the source of it—a very tiny bird. Indeed, the winter wren puts every ounce of its body into its song. Its short tail is often held straight up above its back while it sings.

This year-round resident of coastal areas is thought to be polygamous. Males build several nests and sing to attract mates. The female, drawn by the male's song, inspects a nest before choosing her mate and beginning to nest. All wrens respond readily to squeaking (rather than "pishing") sounds made for the purpose of calling them in.

# Marsh Wren *Cistothorus palustris*

**DESCRIPTION Adult:** Black triangular patch with white stripes on back; breast white; belly buff; eye line white and prominent.
**SIZE** Length to 5" (12.5 cm).
**NESTING Nest:** Attached to cattails, bulrushes or other marsh plants. Nest materials include wet grass, cattails and rushes; nest is lined with grass, plant down and feathers. **Eggs:** Normally 4–5, light brown with dark brown blotches.
**HABITAT** Cattail or rush marshes.

The marsh wren is a songster, and it favors singing sites that are hidden from view. Rarely does the male venture far from such locations. Its distinctive song has been described as everything from a gurgling rattle to a rattling chatter. To view the marsh wren is often difficult—sometimes seemingly impossible. The patient viewer is most likely to be rewarded: eventually the male climbs to a position where he can be seen.

This wren builds distinctive, sphere-shaped covered nests among cattails and rushes. Males have been known to make as many as 20 dummy nests, possibly to impress females, to mark territory or to distract predators from the real nest. Males are also known to be polygynous, mating with as many as 3 females each. This is more likely to occur in areas with abundant insects, the main food of this species.

# American Dipper *Cinclus mexicanus*

**DESCRIPTION** Gray overall with a stocky build.
**SIZE** Length to 6 ½" (16 cm).
**NESTING Nest:** On a rock ledge or among roots on a stream bank, often behind a waterfall. Domed nest is made from mosses, twigs and grass. **Eggs:** Normally 4–5, white.
**HABITAT** Along clear mountain streams.

The American dipper is capable of walking or swimming along the bottoms of fast-moving streams to obtain food. Meals consist primarily of aquatic insect larvae living under stones, as well as insects flying above the water. The water ouzel, as this bird is sometimes called, raises 2 broods per year in parts of its range. It is a year-round resident that often moves down from higher elevations during the winter months, and its continuous push-ups (bobbing) are characteristic.

# Mountain Bluebird *Sialia currucoides*

**DESCRIPTION Male:** Head, back and wings sky blue; breast lighter. **Female:** Wings and tail blue; body gray
**SIZE** Length to 7 ¼" (18 cm).
**NESTING Nest:** In a natural tree cavity or old woodpecker hole. Nest materials include grass, twigs, rootlets, hair and feathers. **Eggs:** Normally 5–6, bluish.
**HABITAT** Open areas with well-spaced trees.

The mountain bluebird is a quiet, gentle member of the bird world. It is a beautiful species, capable of hovering for several seconds while hunting for large insects. Nesting takes place in the holes of trees, often those made by the northern flicker (see p. 64). These birds also readily accept nest boxes in suitable locations. Thousands of such boxes have been set up along various rural roads throughout North America to attract bluebirds, and these bluebird trails have been very successful in attracting tree swallows (p. 65) as well. European starlings (p. 75) and house sparrows (p. 87), however, often take over potential nest sites for this species.

**Similar Species:** The western bluebird (*Sialia mexicana*) is a similar species, easily distinguishable by its orange breast.

# Hermit Thrush *Catharus guttatus*

**DESCRIPTION** Back and wings brown; rump and tail reddish brown.
**SIZE** Length to 7" (18 cm).
**NESTING Nest:** On the ground or in a tree, 3–12' (1–3.5 m) off the ground. Nest materials include twigs, moss, weeds, bark, pine needles and rootlets. **Eggs:** Normally 4, bluish, occasionally with brown speckles.
**HABITAT** Forested areas.

The hermit thrush is well known for its fabulous flute-like song, a series of notes that start at a low pitch and then rise. This song is symbolic of forest life of North America, and considered by some to be the finest birdsong on the continent. The hermit thrush inhabits higher elevations and sometimes winters at lower elevations in mild areas. It is known for its habit of occasionally flicking its tail upward, then slowly lowering it.

**Similar Species:** The Swainson's thrush (*Catharus ustulatus*) is a late migrant that occupies lower elevations and is often found in wetland environments and forest margins. It lacks the reddish brown rump and tail of the hermit thrush.

# American Robin *Turdus migratorius*

**DESCRIPTION** Back and wings gray-brown; breast brick red. **Male:** Head black.
**SIZE** Length to 10" (25 cm).
**NESTING Nest:** In a tree, 5–25' (1.5–8 m) off the ground. Nest materials include grass, twigs and mud. **Eggs:** Normally 4, light blue.
**HABITAT** A wide range of habitats.

For many people, the song of the American robin marks the arrival of spring. This amazing species has adapted well to human environments and often has 3 clutches in one year. It feeds on earthworms, cutworms and many other insects, thriving where many other thrushes have not. In the fall, however, its diet changes considerably to a selection of berries and other fruits. The American robin is a common resident throughout North America, and it winters from southern British Columbia southward. Sometimes individuals are caught in unexpected snowstorms and cannot obtain food. At such times they will eat pieces of apple from a feeder, placed there by people wishing to help them out.

# Varied Thrush *Ixoreus naevius*

*This varied thrush was caught in a snowstorm.*

**DESCRIPTION Male:** Back grayish blue; breast orange with black necklace; eyebrow and wing bars orange. **Female:** Similar to male, back brown and lacking a necklace.
**SIZE** Length to 9 ½" (24 cm).
**NESTING Nest:** In a tree, 5–15' (1.5–4.5 m) off the ground. Nest is made from twigs, moss, leaves, bark and grass. **Eggs:** Normally 3–4, pale blue with light brown speckles.
**HABITAT** Wet coniferous forests.

The varied thrush is known for creating its distinctive sounds of solitude in the woods: a series of long, loud, penetrating notes, each followed by another note about a second later. This is a forest-loving thrush that is often seen stirring up dead leaves while foraging on the ground for food. Its menu changes from a variety of insects in the summer months to seeds and berries in winter. This thrush is normally found at higher elevations, but winter conditions often push them much lower down.

# Cedar Waxwing *Bombycilla cedrorum*

**DESCRIPTION** Brown overall; head with crest; wings gray with red (waxy) spots; tail with yellow (waxy) tip; undertail coverts white; belly yellowish.
**SIZE** Length to 7 ¼" (18 cm).
**NESTING Nest:** In a tree, 6–20' (1.5–6 m) off the ground. Nest materials include twigs, grass, moss and hair. **Eggs:** Normally 3–5, gray with brown spots.
**HABITAT** Open areas where berries are available.

The cedar waxwing, one of only 3 species of waxwings world-wide, delights in dining primarily on seasonal fruits. Waxwings are frugivores (fruit eaters), enjoying mountain ash, raspberry, rose, bearberry and juniper, among other fruits. These berries contribute the carotenoid pigments the birds need to produce the wax-like secretions on their wings and tail tips.

**Similar Species:** The Bohemian waxwing (*Bombycilla garrulus*) is similar in coloration. This winter visitor is a larger bird, with white bars and yellow spots on the wings and cinnamon undertail coverts. It often accompanies the cedar waxwing in winter and breeds in the north.

# European Starling *Sturnus vulgaris*

**DESCRIPTION Adult:** Overall black with white spots (feathers are tipped with white). **Breeding adult:** Body iridescent overall, bill yellow.
**SIZE** Length to 8 ½" (21 cm).
**NESTING Nest:** In a cavity. Nest materials include twigs, grass, leaves and feathers. **Eggs:** Normally 4–6, greenish white or bluish white.
**HABITAT** Farmlands, fields and similar situations; urban settings.

The European starling was introduced to North America over a century ago and is now so common throughout most of the continent that it is regarded as a pest. It is a social species, whose flocks number in the thousands during the winter months. Starlings are aggressive, occupying nesting cavities that would otherwise be used by several native species, and occasionally laying their eggs in the nests of other birds. They are also well known for their ability to mimic the songs and calls of other birds.

# Cassin's Vireo *Vireo cassinii*

**DESCRIPTION** Body greenish; head gray; breast whitish; eyes dark surrounded by distinctive "white spectacles."
**SIZE** Length to 5 ½" (14 cm).
**NESTING Nest:** In a tree, 3–12' (1–3.5 m) off the ground. Nest materials include grass, plant fibers and strips of bark. **Eggs:** Normally 3–5, whitish.
**HABITAT** Deciduous woodlands.

Vireos are treetop dwellers that are often heard but can be difficult to observe. They feed primarily on insects and, in the fall, fruit. Cassin's vireo and two additional species, which occur farther east, were all formerly called the solitary vireo, but now they are understood to be 3 separate species.

**Similar Species:** The red-eyed vireo (*Vireo olivaceus*) is easy to identify if you are close enough to see the eye color. The warbling vireo (*Vireo gilvus*) is a drab, grayish vireo that is known for its warbling song. Hutton's vireo (*Vireo huttoni*) is a smaller species, with a much shorter bill and drab olive-colored underparts.

# Wilson's Warbler *Wilsonia pusilla*

**DESCRIPTION** Back and wings olive; underparts yellow.
**Male:** Cap black; face yellow.
**Female:** Cap sometimes blackish; forehead yellowish.
**SIZE** Length to 4 ¾" (12 cm).
**NESTING Nest:** On the ground or in a shrub or vine, to 3' (1 m) off the ground. Nest materials include leaves, grass and moss; nest is lined with grass and hair. **Eggs:** Normally 4–6, cream-colored with brown markings.
**HABITAT** Moist woods, bogs and thickets.

The Wilson's warbler is a very active species with a habit of twitching its wings and tail while perched. It is a delightful wood warbler and common in moist areas, where it actively pursues a great variety of insects with aerial acrobatics. This bird's song is loud and has been written as *chi chi chi chi chet chet*. Biologists have discovered that populations breeding as far north as Alaska winter in the southern portion of the wintering range, Central America. However, southern breeding populations, such as those in California, winter only as far south as Baja California. It is unknown why this pattern of migration, called leapfrog migration, occurs.

# Yellow Warbler *Dendroica petechia*

**DESCRIPTION Male:** Body yellow; underside streaked with red; eye dark. **Female:** Body yellow; eye dark.
**SIZE** Length to 5" (12.5 cm).
**NESTING Nest:** In a tree or shrub, 2–60' (.5–18 m) off the ground. Nest materials include grass and shredded bark; nest is lined with plant down. **Eggs:** Normally 4–5, whitish with brown and gray speckles.
**HABITAT** Deciduous trees or shrubs.

The brilliant colors of the yellow warbler inspire all who see this bird, and its vibrant song is not soon forgotten. It is a lively song, sometimes described as *sweet-sweet-sweet summer swee*—but it certainly loses something in the translation.

*Male*

This species is sometimes parasitized by the brown-headed cowbird (see p. 83). When a nest is parasitized, the yellow warbler either deserts the nest or builds a new nest over the old one. One nest contained a total of 6 nests, 5 of which contained cowbird eggs. In some areas of North America, as many as 75% of warblers' nests have been parasitized, but studies in the Pacific Northwest indicate that the rate here is closer to 15%.

*Female yellow warbler.*

**Similar Species:** The orange-crowned warbler (*Vermivora celata*) is a common warbler that is often found in shrubby areas. It is olive above and lighter below with streaks on the breast. Its orange crown is not often seen in the field.

# Yellow-rumped Warbler *Dendroica coronata*

**DESCRIPTION Male:** Back, wings and head blue; rump, throat and cap yellow. **Female:** Overall duller in color than the male.
**SIZE** Length to 5 ½" (14 cm).
**NESTING Nest:** In a tree, 4–50' (1–15 m) off the ground. Nest materials include bark, twigs and roots; nest is lined with hair and feathers. **Eggs:** Normally 4–5, cream-colored with brown and gray speckles.
**HABITAT** Treed areas.

The yellow-rumped warbler is a fine-dining insectivore, enjoying ants, wasps, house flies, crane flies, gnats, true bugs and other insects. This very early migrant is also known to feed on some vegetation. In springtime, migrants announce their arrival from their winter homes in South America. Their beautiful and distinctive warble has been described as *seet-seet-seet-seet trrrrr*. These warblers often accompany other species while on migration.

The yellow-rumped warbler can be separated into two groups or subspecies, the "Audubon's warbler" and "myrtle warbler," which were once considered separate species. Breeding males of both species have distinctive plumage. The adult male "Audubon's warbler" displays bright patches of yellow on the crown, throat, side and rump. The adult male "myrtle warbler" displays bright patches of yellow on the crown, side and rump, but has a white throat and eyebrow. Both subspecies can be observed in the Pacific Northwest, but "Audubon's warbler" is more common.

# Common Yellowthroat *Geothlypis trichas*

**DESCRIPTION Male:** Mask black with white border; throat and breast bright yellow; upper parts olive green. **Female:** Face does not have mask; throat and breast yellow; upper parts olive green.
**SIZE** Length to 5" (12.5 cm).
**NESTING Nest:** Near the ground on weeds, grasses and shrubs. Nest materials include weeds, grass, sedges, leaves and bark; nest is lined with grass and hair. **Eggs:** Normally 3–5, whitish with brown and black speckles.
**HABITAT** Wetlands.

A visit to a cattail marsh is not complete until the distinctive voice of the common yellowthroat is heard. Its voice is often described as *whitchity, whitchity, whitchity*, or occasionally as *your money, your money, your money*. Its call sounds like a rubber band—doink. The common yellowthroat also has a flight song in which the male begins singing on a low shrub, then flies to a height of 25–100' (8–30 m) in an undulating pattern, from which it swoops down to a new low perch. The song and various notes are only made on the bird's ascent and at the peak of its display; the descent takes place without calls or song. Males are normally monogamous but in at least one instance a male is known to have had two mates. Brown-headed cowbirds (see p. 83) often deposit their eggs in the nests of this host.

# Western Tanager *Piranga ludoviciana*

**DESCRIPTION Breeding male:** Belly yellow; face red; back black. **Female:** Back gray; head greenish yellow; underparts greenish yellow or gray.
**SIZE** Length to 7" (18 cm).
**NESTING Nest:** In a tree, 15–65' (4.5–20 m) off the ground. Nest is made from twigs, grass and rootlets, and is lined with hair. **Eggs:** Normally 3–5, bluish with brown blotches.
**HABITAT** Conifer forests in summer.

Although the western tanager is a mountain resident, it is often observed in a wide range of other habitats while migrating to its summer residence. The stunning plumage of this bird is memorable. This tanager may also visit feeders to eat fresh fruit, including halved oranges. While nesting, males are often heard singing their robin-like song from a high perch in the forest canopy. The call is distinctive, a quick *prid-a-dit*. The brown-headed cowbird (see p. 83) is known to parasitize the nests of the western tanager with its eggs.

# Spotted Towhee *Pipilo maculatus*

**DESCRIPTION Male:** Hood black; breast white below with chestnut sides; eyes red. **Female:** Colors subdued.
**SIZE** Length to 8 ½" (22 cm).
**NESTING Nest:** On or near the ground. Nest materials include leaves, bark and grasses. **Eggs:** Normally 2–6, cream-colored with brown blotches.
**HABITAT** Forest edges and shrubby areas.

The spotted towhee scratches at the ground using both feet at once, to stir up leaves on the ground in search of food. The cheery *chewink* or *chweee* call of this species can often be heard from ground level before the bird is seen. Males can be heard singing with a high trill as they proclaim their territory from tall shrubs. This sparrow-like bird can be found from southern B.C. to central Guatemala. It was formerly called the rufous-sided towhee, along with a similar species, the eastern towhee (*Pipilo erythrophthalmus*), which lacks spots.

# Savannah Sparrow *Passerculus sandwichensis*

**DESCRIPTION** Eyebrow yellow; breast and sides streaked; back and wings dark brown.
**SIZE** Length to 5 ½" (14 cm).
**NESTING Nest:** On the ground, made from grass, lined with fine grass. **Eggs:** Normally 2–6, whitish with brown speckles.
**HABITAT** Open areas, especially grasslands and wetlands.

This widespread resident may be seen and heard singing on top of a shrub or fence post in open country. Here they nest, going largely undetected until the male proclaims his territory. The male's buzzy "song" may be summarized as *tea tea tea teeeeea today*. The savannah sparrow is a common and widespread species that dines on a variety of foods including seeds, beetles and grasshoppers. Males may have more than one mate, and females have been known to lay eggs in other savannah sparows' nests as well as their own.

# Fox Sparrow *Passerella iliaca*

**DESCRIPTION** Head and back dark brown to dark gray; rump and tail reddish; underparts heavily spotted with a large central blotch; yellow lower mandible (bill).
**SIZE** Length to 7" (18 cm).
**NESTING Nest:** On the ground or in a low shrub or tree, made from grass, weeds and moss, lined with grass. **Eggs:** Normally 2–5, greenish blotched with reddish brown.
**HABITAT** Open shrubby and forest areas.

The fox sparrow is often seen scratching its feet along the ground as it forages for seeds, fruits, insects and various other foods. This species is commonly seen throughout the Pacific Northwest during the warmer months, and is a common year-round resident in coastal areas. It can be found from sea level to subalpine elevations. At low elevations, during the winter, it is especially common in blackberry hedgerows.

**Similar Species:** This common species is easily confused with the song sparrow (p. 81). Both species display spotted underparts and a central breast spot. The fox sparrow is dark overall with a yellow lower mandible and lacks facial markings, while the song sparrow is lighter overall with a gray eyebrow and dark bill.

# Song Sparrow *Melospiza melodia*

**DESCRIPTION** Breast white with dark brown streaks and central spot; eyebrow gray; bill dark.
**SIZE** Length to 6" (15 cm).
**NESTING Nest:** On the ground or in a tree or shrub, to 10' (3 m) off the ground. Nest materials include weeds, grass, bark strips; nest is lined with grass, rootlets and hair. **Eggs:** Normally 4, whitish with reddish brown blotches.
**HABITAT** Dense shrubby areas.

This sparrow is a very common resident and visitor throughout much of the Pacific Northwest, from the beach to the mountaintops. Its song is rich and varied, beginning with a *sweet, sweet, sweet* and followed by a trill or warble. It has also been said to sing *hip-hip-hooray boys, springs here!*—an appropriate phrase, since this sparrow begins its nesting activities as early as April in coastal areas. This bird's song is so distinctive that it is embedded in both its common name and its scientific name, melodia ("singing" or "song").

The song sparrow feeds primarily on seeds and insects, which makes it an important factor in the natural control of weed seeds and injurious insects. Adults may nest more than once during the season, and in fact there is one record of a pair successfully raising 4 broods in one season, the last nest also containing 2 eggs of the brown-headed cowbird (p. 83).

# White-crowned Sparrow *Zonotrichia leucophrys*

**DESCRIPTION** Crown black and white striped; throat gray; wings and back brown.
**SIZE** Length to 7" (18 cm).
**NESTING Nest:** On the ground or in a low shrub, made from grass, twigs, rootlets and bark, and lined with grass, feathers and hair. **Eggs:** Normally 4–5, whitish to greenish with reddish brown speckles.
**HABITAT** Dense shrubby areas.

The spring arrival of the white-crowned sparrow is a welcome sight after the quiet winter months. It is a common year-round resident in the Pacific Northwest, from sea level to alpine elevations. This sparrow feeds on seeds, insects and occasionally fruit and buds. Its song is vibrant and quite variable, and has been written out as *more-wet-wetter-chee-zee* or the undignified *I I I gotta go wee-wee now*. The white-crowned sparrow often nests in close proximity to humans in both urban and rural settings, including urban residential backyards, orchards, clearcut areas and farmlands.

# Dark-eyed Junco *Junco hyemalis*

**DESCRIPTION "Oregon" form Male:** Back reddish brown; hood black; breast white; outer tail feathers white. **"Oregon" form Female:** Colors drab overall.
**SIZE** Length to 6 ¼" (16 cm).
**NESTING Nest:** On the ground. Nest built from grass and leaves, lined with fine grass, hair and feathers. **Eggs:** Normally 3–5, whitish with brown and gray markings.
**HABITAT** A wide variety of habitats.

The coloration of the dark-eyed junco varies considerably across North America, where several forms (subspecies) occur. The "Oregon" form, from the West, is darker and was once considered a separate species. Other forms lack the black hood, and in one other form the bird's back is gray. This year-round resident is a regular visitor to bird feeders over the winter months. The cheery presence of the dark-eyed junco is always a welcome sight!

*Male sings on territory.*

# Red-winged Blackbird *Agelaius phoeniceus*

**DESCRIPTION Male:** Body black; shoulder patches red edged with yellow. **Female:** Brown overall; heavily streaked below.
**SIZE** Length to 8 ¾" (22 cm).
**NESTING Nest:** Attached to cattails, bulrushes or willows. Nest materials include grass, reeds and leaves; nest is lined with grasses. **Eggs:** Normally 3–4, greenish with brown blotches.
**HABITAT** Wetlands.

The colorful red-winged blackbird has been declared the most abundant land bird in North America, with winter numbers in the United States alone estimated at an astounding 190 million. It is a common and colorful resident, often found in the company of the marsh wren (see p. 72) in spring and summer. The red-winged blackbird is a very vocal species, with a repertoire of many "songs," calls and notes, including *conc-a-ree or okalee*, as well as *eat my cheeeses*. Its calls include *chuck* and a metallic *kink*.

# Brown-headed Cowbird *Molothrus ater*

**DESCRIPTION Male:** Head dark brown; body metallic black. **Female:** Overall light brown; breast streaked.
**SIZE** Length to 7 ½" (19 cm).
**NESTING Nest:** None; eggs are laid in other species' nests. **Eggs:** Have been known to lay 70 or more in one season, whitish with brown blotches.
**HABITAT** Rangeland, clearcuts, forest edges and other open habitats.

This common species lays its eggs in the nests of other birds. It has developed several adaptations that make it an effective parasite. The female can lay an egg in a host's nest in less than one minute, while a non-parasitic species requires 21 to 104 minutes. As well, the female cowbird lays an average of 40 eggs during one breeding season, while most perching birds lay 4–6 per clutch. Cowbirds' eggs also require less time to hatch than most species. Not all hosts accept this intruder's egg, however. Among the many responses are to eject the egg outright, to abandon the nest altogether or to construct a new nest over the parasitized one. The brown-headed cowbird is known to parasitize 226 species of birds in North America.

*Male.*

*Cowbirds are often found near bison and cattle.*

# Evening Grosbeak *Coccothraustes vespertinus*

**DESCRIPTION Male:** Belly and rump yellow; head dark with yellow eyebrow; wings black and white; bill massive. **Female:** Tan overall; wings black with white patches.
**SIZE** Length to 8" (20 cm).
**NESTING Nest:** In a tree, 10–100' (3–30 m) off the ground. Nest is made from twigs, and lined with grasses, moss and pine needles. **Eggs:** Normally 3–4, bluish with brown blotches.
**HABITAT** Mixed and coniferous woods.

The striking colors of the evening grosbeak often cause a great commotion when the birds are viewed for the first time at a feeder. These birds' insatiable appetite for sunflower seeds in winter is truly remarkable. They also feed on the fruit of saskatoon, chokecherry and pin cherry in season, removing the "useless" pulp to get at the seeds inside. This bird can apply a pressure of 110 lbs (50 kg) with its powerful bill to crack the shells of its food. It is a year-round resident that breeds in mixed woods, and often at higher elevations in the mountains as well. Populations of evening grosbeak fluctuate greatly from year to year.

# House Finch *Carpodacus mexicanus*

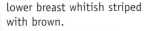

**DESCRIPTION Male:** Cap, back and wings brown; bib, front of head and rump red; undertail coverts and lower breast whitish striped with brown. **Female:** Overall light brown; breast streaked.
**SIZE** Length to 6" (15 cm).
**NESTING Nest:** In many situations, including in trees and in holes in structures, 12–15' (3.5–4.5 m) off the ground. Nest is made from grass, twigs, string and feathers. **Eggs:** Normally 4–5, bluish with black and lavender markings.
**HABITAT** Sunny, open, dry areas.

*Male.*

*Female.*

The house finch is a common year-round resident in much of the Pacific Northwest. It enjoys a meal of fresh fruit, such as the native Pacific crabapple (*Malus fusca*), but unfortunately it is also fond of cultivated fruits. This inclination sometimes gets house finches into a wee bit of trouble, especially since they are gregarious and often accumulate in large numbers in the fall.

**Similar Species:** The purple finch (*Carpodacus purpureus*) is a very similar species, but it lacks the brown cap and its undertail coverts are not usually streaked.

# Pine Grosbeak *Pinicola enucleator*

**DESCRIPTION Male:** Gray overall; head, back and underparts tipped with pink. **Female and juvenile:** Gray overall; head, rump and underparts orange.
**SIZE** Length to 9" (23 cm).
**NESTING Nest:** In a conifer, 5–15' (1.5–4.5 m) off the ground. Nest materials include twigs and rootlets; nest is lined with grasses, lichens and moss. **Eggs:** Normally 2–5, green with brown, purple and black speckles.
**HABITAT** Open coniferous woods.

The pine grosbeak is a colorful resident throughout much of the Pacific Northwest. It appears in abundance in some years and not at all in others, perhaps because of variations in weather or food supply. Its diet includes the fruit of crabapples and the seeds of various conifers, and it is occasionally seen at feeding stations. These birds are seed-lovers, especially fond of sunflower seeds—in fact, their presence is often associated with abundant seed crops. They are believed to nest in subalpine forests, but only a few nests have ever been found. During the winter, the birds move to lower elevations.

*Female.*

*Male.*

# Gray-crowned Rosy-finch *Leucosticte tephrocotis*

**DESCRIPTION Male:** Dark brown overall; wings and flanks pinkish brown; back of head gray. **Female:** Dark brown overall; back of head gray. **SIZE** Length to 6" (15 cm). **NESTING Nest:** Among boulders. Nest materials include grass, rootlets, lichens and moss; nest is lined with grass, feathers and hair. **Eggs:** Normally 4–5, white with reddish brown speckles. **HABITAT** Rocky alpine areas.

The gray-crowned rosy-finch is a summer resident of the high alpine, and is observed in the company of the white-tailed ptarmigan (see p. 39). It feeds on seeds, berries and insects tucked away in the sparse vegetation. Because it nests in crevices on rock cliffs, this species encounters little competition in its chosen habitat. While on migration, individuals have been observed from sea level and alpine elevations. They accumulate in large flocks while migrating. These flocks have been documented to number from several hundred to 3,000 individuals.

# Common Redpoll *Carduelis flammea*

**DESCRIPTION Breeding male:** Brown with prominent streaking; breast and forehead rose-colored. **Female:** Similar to male, but the breast lacks the rosy color. **SIZE** Length to 5 ¼" (13 cm). **NESTING Nest:** In low shrubs, near the ground. Nest materials include fine twigs, grass and moss; nest is lined with feathers. **Eggs:** Normally 4–5, pale green to bluish green. **HABITAT** Birch trees, shrubby and weedy areas.

"Nomadic" best describes the life of the common redpoll. Flocks are often observed during the winter, feeding in seed trees, especially birch trees. They will also stop and eat at a feeder if sunflower and niger (thistle) seeds are available. This is a hardy species that moves south from its Arctic summer range each year, but numbers and ranges fluctuate greatly from year to year. Some years they seem to be everywhere; other years they are rarely observed. Food supplies, temperature and snow do not seem to be factors in these fluctuations.

# American Goldfinch *Carduelis tristis*

**DESCRIPTION Summer male:** Body yellow; cap and tail black; wings black with white bars. **Summer female:** Body yellowish brown; wings black. **Winter male:** Body yellowish brown; head yellowish. **Winter female:** Body yellowish brown; wings black.
**SIZE** Length to 5" (12.5 cm).
**NESTING Nest:** In a tree or shrub. Nest is compact and well made from plant fibers, spider webs and plant down. **Eggs:** Normally 4–6, bluish white, occasionally with brown speckles.
**HABITAT** Weedy areas and open spaces.

The American goldfinch is primarily a seed eater, favoring the seeds of thistle, dandelion and similar plants. It is a striking species, which also feeds on insects during the summer and dines on smaller seeds at feeders. During the courtship display, the male conducts an exaggerated loop flight while singing his *perchicoree* call. The brown-headed cowbird (see p. 83), which lays its eggs in the nests of many other birds in the Pacific Northwest, is discouraged by the American goldfinch. Its grain diet has been found to retard the growth of young cowbirds, and as a result they are unable to fledge.

# House Sparrow *Passer domesticus*

**DESCRIPTION Breeding male:** Crown gray; nape chestnut; bib black. **Female:** Back streaked; eye-stripe buff.
**SIZE** Length to 6 ¼" (15.5 cm).
**NESTING Nest:** In a cavity, in the nest of other birds. Nest materials include grass, weeds and twigs; nest is lined with feathers. **Eggs:** Normally 3–6, whitish with brown and gray blotches.
**HABITAT** Farms, towns and cities.

The house sparrow, or English sparrow as it is often called, is an introduced member of the weaver finch family that is now common throughout most of North America. It finds an occupied cavity to nest in, then removes the eggs, evicts the adults and kills the young of the resident species. The house sparrow dines on a wide range of foods, including insects, spiders, small fruit, weed seeds, grain and crumbs, and it frequents bird feeders as well. Over the past few years, this species has declined in numbers, due to a reduction in available nest sites.

*Female.*

# Glossary

**accipiter:** a forest hawk belonging to the genus *Accipiter*.

**altricial:** referring to hatching that occurs at an early stage of the chick's development.

**buteo:** a hawk belonging to the genus *Buteo*.

**conifer:** an evergreen tree that bears needles.

**crepuscular:** active before dawn and after dusk.

**deciduous:** trees that lose their leaves annually.

**diurnal:** active during daylight hours.

**insectivore:** feeding on insects.

**mandible:** lower jaw or bill.

**nocturnal:** active during darkness.

**omnivorous:** feeding on both animals and plants.

**parasitic:** referring to a close relationship in which one species benefits at the expense of another.

**polyandry:** a mating practice in which a female mates with more than one male, but each male mates with only one female.

**polygyny:** a mating practice in which one male mates with more than one female, but each female mates with only one male.

**precocial:** referring to hatching that occurs at a late stage of the chick's development.

**primary feathers:** the elongated feathers on the last segment of the wing.

**riparian:** pertaining to or along the edge of a river or stream.

**scapular:** referring to the shoulder area.

**speculum:** trailing edge of secondary feathers.

# For Further Reading

## BIRDS

Baron, Nancy & John Acorn. 1997. *Birds of Coastal British Columbia*. Lone Pine Publishing, Edmonton, AB

Campbell, R. Wayne et al. 1990-2001. *The Birds of British Columbia*, Volumes 1-4. UBC Press, Vancouver, BC

Dunne, Pete, D. Sibley, & C. Sutton. 1988. *Hawks in Flight: The Flight Identification of North American Migrant Raptors*. Houghton Mifflin Company. Boston, MA.

Johnsgard, Paul A. 1988. *North American Owls: Biology and Natural History*. Smithsonian Institution Press, Washington, DC

Kaufman, Kenn. 1996. *Lives of North American Birds*. Houghton Mifflin Co. Boston, MA

Ritchison, Gary. 1999. *Wild Bird Guides: Downy Woodpecker*. Stackpole Books, Mechanicsburg, PA

## FEEDERS, BIRDHOUSES & ATTRACTING BIRDS

Gerhards, Paul. 1999. *Birdhouses & Feeders You Can Make: Complete Plans and Instructions for Bird-Friendly Nesting and Feeding Sites*. Stackpole Books, Mechanicsburg, PA

Laubach, R. & C. M. Laubach, 1998. *Backyard Birdhouse Book: Building Nestboxes and Creating Natural Habitats*. Story Books, Pownal, VT

Merilees, Bill. 2000. *The New Gardening For Wildlife: A Guide for Nature Lovers*. Whitecap Books, Vancouver, BC

Troops, Connie. 1994. *Bluebirds Forever*. Voyageur Press, Inc. Stillwater, MN

# Acknowledgments

I would like to thank the many people who assisted with this project.

Mary Schendlinger for her careful editing.

Kevin MacPherson for insightful scientific editing, graciously conducted.

Louise Waterhouse for her thoughtful comments and suggestions.

Jim Salt, who generously aided me in photographing birds and locating species for photography.

The staff at various national, provincial and state parks throughout British Columbia, Washington and Oregon, who helped locate species for photography.

The skilled photographers who provided photos. Their names appear below.

## Photo Credits

# Index

# About the Author

Duane Sept is a biologist, freelance writer and professional photographer. His biological work has included research on various wildlife species and service as a park naturalist. His photographs have been published internationally, in displays and in books, magazines and other publications, for clients that include BBC Wildlife, Parks Canada, Nature Canada, National Wildlife Federation and World Wildlife Fund.

Today Duane brings a wealth of information to the public as an author, in much the same way he has inspired hundreds of visitors to Canada's parks. His published books include The Beachcomber's Guide to Seashore Life in the Pacific Northwest (Harbour Publishing) and Common Wildflowers of British Columbia (Calypso Publishing). He lives on the Sunshine Coast of British Columbia.